NATIONAL GEOGRAPHIC

FIELD GUIDE TO

BIRDS

FLORIDA

 NATIONAL GEOGRAPHIC

FIELD GUIDE TO

BIRDS

Edited by MEL BAUGHMAN

National Geographic
Washington, D.C.

Introduction

Florida is a birder's paradise. More birds—491 species as of August 2004—have been seen in Florida than in any other state east of the Mississippi River. Because much of the state is subtropical, birding is excellent nearly year-round.

The 125 primary species featured in this guide represent a cross-section of Florida's birding opportunities. Many species such as Brown Pelican are abundant, while others such as White-tailed Kite are rare; some like Blue-winged Teal are widespread, while others such as Red-cockaded Woodpecker are local. There are birds found throughout the continent (Great Blue Heron) and others (Florida Scrub-Jay) found nowhere else in the world.

The diversity of Florida's habitats—more than 80 natural communities—and its conservation ethic—more than one-quarter of the state's land area is under protection in perpetuity—assure the birder an abundance of prime birding areas, including Gulf Islands National Seashore, St. Marks' National Wildlife Refuge, J.N. "Ding" Darling National Wildlife Refuge, the Florida Keys, and the magnificent Dry Tortugas National Park—a series of five small coral and sand keys located about 70 miles west of Key West, accessible solely by private boat or seaplane.

The most diverse birding site is Everglades National Park, with its over 1.5 million acres at Florida's tip. Some 350 species have been observed here. The numbers of wading birds found year round and the shorebirds during winter, can be enormous. And there is the rare surprise: The Cape Sable race of the Seaside Sparrow, included in this guide, is found only here and in adjoining Big Cypress National Preserve. Come, enjoy the wonders for yourself.

BILL PRANTY
Author, *A Birder's Guide to Florida*

CONTENTS

WELCOME TO BIRDING

Early in my birding career, as I moved along an elevated walkway in Everglades National Park, I noticed a shadow flash across the surface of the pond. Lofting above me was one of the most extraordinary sights I had ever seen: a stark-white and velvet-black raptor twirling in an airborne ballet. The Swallow-tailed Kite. Enchanted, I became a dedicated birder on the spot. This elegant flyer was my "spark-bird," the bird that trips one into a lifelong passion of birding.

I have been birding across America for 30 years, and continue to find surprises like this everywhere I go. My bible— as it is for many—has been the *National Geographic Field Guide to the Birds of North America,* a complete field reference to the more than 800 species of birds that occur on the continent.

While visiting separate regions and states, I have longed for a compact version of that guide—one I could carry in my pocket or backpack that would offer a quick reference to the birds I am most likely to see during a day in the field, and that would help birders I meet who are just getting started.

Here it is. This photographic guide to birds of Florida is designed to give birders of all levels an easy reference to the most commonly seen birds: What they look like at a glance, how they act, where they live, and where you can find them. The birds are listed in order of their families, as prescribed by the American Ornithologists' Union, an order used in the best field guides in the world. Before long, you will be comfortable with the family concept, and this newly acquired knowledge will aid you in your birding career. But, because finding birds *fast* is key in the field, there are two "quick reference" indexes—based on color and on alphabet.

Together, the carefully combined elements of this guide will start you on a lifelong journey of wonder and surprise.

MEL BAUGHMAN
Editor

National Geographic's *Field Guide to Birds: Florida* is designed to help birders at any level quickly identify birds in the field. The book is organized by bird families, following the order in the *Checklist to the Birds of North America* by the American Ornithologists' Union. Families share structural characteristics. By learning these early, birders will establish a basis for a lifetime of identifying birds and related family members. (For quick reference in the field, use the color and alphabetical indexes at the back.)

A family may have one member or dozens of members, or species. In this book each family is identified in English, the common name. Each species is also identified in English, and by its Latin genus and species, its scientific name. One species is featured in each entry. An entry begins with Field Marks, the physical clues used to quickly identify a bird, such as body shape and size, bill length, and eye and plumage color. A bird's body parts yield vital clues to identification so a birder needs to

Least Flycatcher

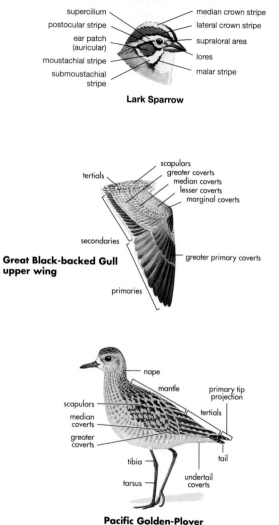

Lark Sparrow

supercilium
postocular stripe
ear patch (auricular)
moustachial stripe
submoustachial stripe
median crown stripe
lateral crown stripe
supraloral area
lores
malar stripe

Great Black-backed Gull upper wing

tertials
scapulars
greater coverts
median coverts
lesser coverts
marginal coverts
secondaries
greater primary coverts
primaries

Pacific Golden-Plover

nape
mantle
primary tip projection
tertials
scapulars
median coverts
greater coverts
tibia
tarsus
undertail coverts
tail

become familiar with them. After the first glance at body type, take note of the head shape and markings, such as stripes, eye rings, and crown. Bill shape and color are next. Then body and wing details: wing bars, color of primary flight feathers, wing color at rest, and shape and markings when extended in flight. Tail shape, length, color, and banding play a big part, too. Below is a key to using this informative guide.

NORTHERN BOBWHITE

Colinus virginianus L. 9.5" (25 cm)

FIELD MARKS
Mottled reddish brown quail with short gray tail

Striped, reddish brown flanks

Throat and eye stripe white in male, buff-colored in female

Juvenile is smaller and duller

Behavior
Male's call is rising, whistled *bob-white*, heard chiefly in late spring and summer. A whistled *hoy* call can be heard year-round. A ground feeder, it forages for seeds, grains, insects, and leaf buds. Feeds and roosts in a covey except during nesting season. Both male and female help build the nest. Nest may be a hollow trampled down in a clump of tall grass, but is more often a woven cover of pine needles, grass, and vegetation with an opening on one side.

Habitat
The Bobwhite has the largest range of all North American quail. It prefers farmland and open woodlands with plentiful underbrush. Also frequents suburban backyard feeders.

Local Sites
Not considered migratory, the Bobwhite remains localized and breeds in the preferred habitat. Found throughout the state but particularly common in northern Florida.

FIELD NOTES: To keep warm at night, a covey of Bobwhites will roost on the ground in a circle, with heads to guard and bodies inward, touching. When alarmed, a Northern Bobwhite is more likely to run than to fly.

Year-round | Adult male

❶ Beneath the **Common Name** is the **Latin**, or **Scientific, Name** Beside it is the bird's length, and frequently wingspan. Wingspan occurs with birds that are often seen flying.
❷ **Field Marks:** Gives basic field identification for body, head and bill shape, and markings.
❸ **Range Map:** Shows year-round range in purple, breeding range in red, winter range in blue. Breeding colony shown by a black dot.
❹ **Behavior:** A step beyond **Field Marks,** gives clues to identifying a bird's habits, such as feeding, flight pattern, personality, courtship, nest-building, and songs and calls.
❺ **Habitat:** Reveals the area it most inhabits, such as forested regions, marshy areas, cities, or farms.

May include nesting sites.
❻ **Local Sites:** Gives the bird's ranges and local spots to look for it.
❼ **Photograph:** Shows bird in its habitat. May be a female or male adult, or a juvenile. Plumage is breeding, molting, or winter.
❽ **Caption:** Defines the featured bird's age and plumage. If a subspecies, the Latin name is given.
❾ **Field Note:** A special entry that may give a unique point of identification, or compare two species of the same family, or compare two from different families that look alike, or focus on a historic or conservation fact.
❿ **Band:** Gives the common name of the bird's family.

Year-round | Adult

FULVOUS WHISTLING-DUCK

Dendrocygna bicolor L 20" (51 cm)

FIELD MARKS
Rich tawny color overall

Dark back with tawny edges

Female has a dark, continuous
stripe on back of neck

Dark stripe on back of male's
neck is usually broken

Behavior
More active at dusk and night than during the day,
often traveling in large, noisy flocks from roosts to
feeding areas. Feeds both by dabbling and by diving
for aquatic plants and seeds. Stretches out its neck
and legs for landing, more like a swan or goose than
a duck.

Habitat
Forages in rice fields and in shallow, marshy fields
especially associated with agricultural operations as
well as in open country and coastal plains. Known
to perch in trees, as indicated by its former English
common name, the "tree duck."

Local Sites
Often abundant in late summer and early fall in
flooded farm fields in the Zellwood area north of
Lake Apopka and near Belle Glade just south of
Lake Okeechobee.

FIELD NOTES The Black-bellied Whistling-
Duck, *Dendrocygna autumnalis* (inset), a
close relative of the Fulvous Whistling-Duck,
is easily identifiable by its red bill, gray face,
tawny breast, and black belly, tail, and rump. Its white wing
patch shows as a broad white stripe in flight.

Year-round | Adult *canadensis*

CANADA GOOSE

Branta canadensis   L 25"-45" (64 cm-114 cm) W 50"-68" (120 cm)

FIELD MARKS

Black head and neck marked with distinctive white chin strap

In flight, shows large, dark wings, white undertail coverts, white U-shaped rump band

Pale breast color

Behavior

This most common and familiar goose is usually known for migrating in large V-formations. Its distinctive musical call of *honk-a-lonk* makes it easy to identify even without seeing it. Also makes a murmuring sound when feeding and a hissing sound when protecting nest or young.

Habitat

Prefers wetlands, grasslands, and cultivated fields within commuting distance of water. Breeds in open or forested areas near water. It has adapted successfully to man-made habitats such as golf courses and farms, to the extent that it sometimes chases off other nesting waterbirds.

Local Sites

Winters in the northern panhandle of Florida, from the Atlantic coast to the Gulf Coast. Look for this species year-round in extreme northern counties along the Atlantic coast.

FIELD NOTES There are at least ten different subspecies of Canada Goose. Varying in breast coloration, they are generally paler in the eastern U.S. and darker toward the West. They vary in size as well, but generally are smaller in the North and West and larger in the South and East.

Year-round | Adult male domesticated

MUSCOVY DUCK

Cairina moschata L 26"-33" (66 cm-84 cm)

FIELD MARKS
Bulky, blackish duck

Green and purple gloss above

White patches on upper- and underwing

Male has black to reddish knob at base of bill, bare facial skin

Behavior
The wild Muscovy Duck is shy and usually silent. It has sharp claws for perching in trees but is most often seen in slow, gooselike flight at dawn and dusk.

Habitat
Muscovies prefer to nest in tree cavities or man-made nest boxes.

Local Sites
A tropical species of perching duck, the Muscovy was brought from Mexico and Central America. A nest box program in northeastern Mexico helped spread this duck to the Rio Grande area. Now found near Falcon Dam, Texas, it is most populous in southern Texas but occasionally spotted in Florida. Tame escaped birds can be found in parks across North America.

FIELD NOTES Domestic male tends to have a brighter red knob at the base of the bill. Can also be all-white. Female is smaller, duller. Found primarily in Central America, the Muscovy Duck's name may refer to the Muscovy Company, a 16th-century English trading group. The duck's Spanish name, *pato real* (royal duck), took hold when conquistadores presented the ducks to King Phillip II of Spain.

Breeding | Adult male

WOOD DUCK

Aix sponsa L 18½" (47 cm)

FIELD MARKS
Distinctive glossy green plumage,
large crest, reddish eye in male

Short crest, large white teardrop-
shaped eye patch in female

Juvenile resembles female but is
spotted below

Behavior
Most commonly feeds by picking insects from the
water's surface or by tipping into shallows to pluck
invertebrates from the bottom. Wood Duck hens are
known to hatch up to eight eggs in abandoned nests,
or "dump nests," where as many as two dozen "cold"
eggs have been left behind. The omnivorous Wood
Duck's diet changes throughout the year depending
upon available foods and its need for particular
proteins or minerals during migration, breeding,
and molting.

Habitat
Prefers woodlands and forested swamps and can be
seen year-round throughout Florida. Nests in tree
cavities or man-made nest boxes.

Local Sites
Like other perching ducks, the Wood Duck can be seen
perching in trees. It is especially common in open
woodlands near water.

FIELD NOTES Males give off a soft, upslurred whistle when
swimming. Female Wood Ducks have a distinctive rising,
squealing flight call of *oo-eek*. Males molt to a drab eclipse
plumage, still retaining their distinctive head feather pattern
and bill colors.

Year-round | Adult males *carolinensis*

GREEN-WINGED TEAL

Anas crecca L 14½" (37 cm)

FIELD MARKS
Male's chestnut head has dark
green ear patch outlined in white

Female has smaller bill than that
of other female teals; also white
undertail coverts, mottled flanks

In flight, shows green speculum
bordered in buff on leading edge

Behavior
An agile and fast-moving flier, this is the smallest
species of ducks known as dabblers. Dabblers either
take food from the water's surface or up-end, tail in
the air and head submerged, to reach aquatic plants,
seeds, and snails. The Green-winged has a specialized
bill for filtering food from the mud. Travels in small
flocks that synchronize their twists and turns midair.

Habitat
In summer, prefers open country near shallow
freshwater lakes and marshes. Also found on coastal
estuaries and tidal marshes and on shallow lakes and
ponds inland, especially those covered with standing
or floating vegetation. Nests are well hidden among
grasses and weeds, within 200 feet of water.

Local Sites
Found throughout Florida in abundant numbers from
late August through April.

FIELD NOTES The Green-winged Teal tends to remain further
north in the winter than other teals. Pairs usually arrive at
breeding grounds having already mated. In mating rituals, the
male can be seen rearing up out of the water, arching his head
forward and down, shaking his bill rapidly in the water while
giving a sharp whistle.

Breeding | Adult female, left; Adult males, right

MALLARD

Anas platyrhynchos L 23" (58 cm)

FIELD MARKS

Male has metallic green head and
neck, white collar, chestnut breast

Female has mottled brown
plumage, orange bill marked
with black

Both have white tails, underwings

Behavior

A dabbler, the Mallard feeds by picking insects from
the water's surface or by tipping into shallows and
plucking invertebrates and grasses from the bottom.
Male's courtship display includes dipping his bill into
water and bringing it up smartly. The Mallard springs
directly into flight with no running start to take off.
Hybridizes with other species of dabbler, such as the
Mottled Duck and the American Black Duck.

Habitat

This wide-ranging duck nests in northern latitudes
around the globe, preferring freshwater shallows and,
in winter, salt marshes.

Local Sites

The domestic Mallard copes well with man-made
habitats. May be found feeding in marinas and breeding in backyards. Resides throughout
most of Florida.

FIELD NOTES The Mallard has a closely
related cousin, the Mottled Duck, *Anas
fulvigula* (inset), which lives on the southern
coastal plain and does not migrate. Its plumage resembles the
female Mallard's but is darker, with no white on the tail or black
on the bill.

Breeding | Adult male

BLUE-WINGED TEAL

Anas discors L 15½" (39 cm)

FIELD MARKS
Male has violet-gray head, white crescent on sides, white flank patch, light blue forewing patches

Female has spotted undertail coverts, yellowish legs

Bolder facial markings and longer bill than Green-winged Teal

Behavior
Flies rapidly in tight flocks. A dabbling duck, it feeds on surface insects or tips into water to eat aquatic plants, seeds, and small crustaceans. Known to take a toll on the crops of southern rice farmers, the Blue-winged Teal uses its hardened upper mandible to strip grain from the stalk. Like other dabblers, also called "puddle ducks," does not require a running start to take off, but can spring directly into flight.

Habitat
This wide-ranging bird regularly migrates for breeding as far north as Alaska and winters as far south as Colombia. Prefers freshwater marshes, ponds, and lakes in open country. Often seen nesting in dry wetland basins.

Local Sites
Can be spotted in the Arthur R. Marshall Loxahatchee National Wildlife Refuge, northwest of Boca Raton.

FIELD NOTES The Blue-winged Teal tends to be the last bird to reach nesting grounds and the first to leave. In flight, the wing pattern of both male and female matches that of the Cinnamon Teal, whose solid brown body still distinguishes it.

Year-round | Adult male

NORTHERN BOBWHITE

Colinus virginianus L 9¾" (25 cm)

FIELD MARKS

Mottled reddish brown quail with short gray tail

Striped, reddish brown flanks

Throat and eye stripe white in male, buff-colored in female

Juvenile is smaller and duller

Behavior

Male's call is a rising, whistled *bob-white*, heard chiefly in late spring and summer. A whistled *hoy* call can be heard year-round. A ground feeder, it forages for seeds, grains, insects, and leaf buds. Feeds and roosts in a covey except during nesting season. Both male and female help build the nest. Nest may be a hollow trampled down in a clump of tall grass, but is more often a woven cover of pine needles, grass, and vegetation with an opening on one side.

Habitat

The Bobwhite has the largest range of all North American quail. It prefers farmland and open woodlands with plentiful underbrush. Also frequents suburban backyard feeders.

Local Sites

Not considered migratory, the Bobwhite remains localized and breeds in its preferred habitats. Found throughout the state but particularly common in northern Florida.

FIELD NOTES To keep warm at night, a covey of Bobwhites will roost on the ground in a circle, with heads outward and bodies inward, touching. When alarmed, a Northern Bobwhite is more likely to run than to fly.

Year-round | Adult male *silvestris*

WILD TURKEY

Meleagris gallopavo L 37"-46" (94 cm-117 cm)

FIELD MARKS

Male has dark purple, green, and bronze iridescent plumage

Bald, reddish head with fleshy red eye patches; red wattle

Male has black chest feathers

Female smaller, buff-colored

Behavior

Considered a ground feeder, the Wild Turkey will also nest in trees at night. It can fly well for short distances, and will when alarmed, but prefers to walk or run. Male's characteristic display during breeding season involves puffing out its chest, swelling its wattles, spreading its tail, and rattling its wings, all while gobbling and strutting. Male gobbling call may be heard in spring from a mile away.

Habitat

Largest of game birds but shy, the turkey lives communally in small family flocks. Frequents open forests and feeds on seeds, nuts, acorns, and insects found in grain fields and forest edges. Females raise a large brood, nesting in leaf-lined hollows in brush or woodlands.

Local Sites

Look for the Wild Turkey in the Myakka River State Park and in many fields and forested areas throughout the state. Especially seen along country roadsides.

FIELD NOTES Like other game birds, the Wild Turkey has a crop, a food storage pouch that allows it to quickly eat, then hide from predators. The food stays in the crop and is digested later with the aid of grit and pebbles in the gizzard.

Breeding | Adult with chick

COMMON LOON

Gavia immer L 32" (81 cm)

FIELD MARKS

Large loon with thick bill, slightly curved culmen

Breeding plumage lightens, especially head and neck

Steep forehead, crown peaked in front

Behavior

The Common Loon keeps its head level at all times. Its loud yodeling call may be heard year-round, most often on breeding grounds in spring and summer. A diving bird, it prefers a diet of fish up to 10" long, which it harpoons with its pointed beak. Forages by diving and swimming underwater, propelled mainly by its large, paddle-shaped feet. It can stay submerged for up to three minutes at depths of up to 250 feet. It is nearly impossible for the Common Loon to walk on land.

Habitat

Nests on large wooded lakes. Winters in coastal waters or inland on large, ice-free bodies of water. Migrates overland as well as coastally.

Local Sites

Prefers bodies of water with ample room for takeoff. Look for it along state coastlines and, during migratory season, on freshwater lakes in the interior of the northern half of the state.

FIELD NOTES In the fall all loons abandon the northern lakes and head for warmer water. While most species prefer to fly low across water while migrating, the Common Loon flies quite high in the air, beating wings more slowly than its relatives.

Breeding | Adult

PIED-BILLED GREBE

Podilymbus podiceps L 13½" (34 cm)

FIELD MARKS
Short-necked, big-headed, stocky

Breeding adult brown overall

Black ring around stout, whitish bill; black chin and throat

Winter birds lose bill ring; chin becomes white

Behavior
The most common of North American grebes, yet seldom seen on land or in flight. When alarmed, it slowly sinks into the water, holding only its head above the surface. Like most grebes, it eats feathers, perhaps to protect its stomach lining from fish bones.

Habitat
Prefers nesting around freshwater marshes and ponds. Also found in the more open waters of large bays and rivers, where it dives to feed on aquatic insects, small fish, frogs, and vegetable matter.

Local Sites
Found year-round throughout Florida, on freshwater lakes, marshes, and ponds.

FIELD NOTES One of seven species of grebe in North America, the Horned Grebe, *Podiceps auritus* (inset), has breeding plumage distinguished by chestnut foreneck and golden "horns." It breeds on lakes and ponds and winters on ice-free lakes. Another relative, the Eared Grebe, *Podiceps nigricollis*, is a regular winter visitor to Florida, found on freshwater lakes. Its winter plumage resembles the Pied-billed Grebe's.

Year-round | Adult female

MAGNIFICENT FRIGATEBIRD

Fregata magnificens L 40" (102 cm) W 90" (229 cm)

FIELD MARKS

Long, forked tail with long, narrow wings

Male is glossy black with orange throat that turns bright red when inflated in courtship display

Female is blackish brown with white on underparts, red legs

Behavior

The long, graceful wings of the Frigatebird enable it to glide for hours on end with hardly a movement. Feeds by skimming fish and squid from surface of water with great precision or by agilely catching in midair the food it has forced other birds of flight to disgorge. During mating season, the all-black male inflates his gular, or throat, sac, which turns from orange to bright red in courtship display.

Habitat

Generally flies along coastline but wanders casually inland, especially after storms. Nests on small islands, usually those with a dense growth of mangroves or other trees or shrubs. Female constructs a twig nest for a single egg.

Local Sites

Catch these amazing soaring birds during breeding season in the Dry Tortugas. Year-round, watch for them along the southern Florida coastline. Summertime sightings in northern Florida and along the Gulf Coast are not uncommon.

FIELD NOTES The feathers of the Magnificent Frigatebird actually weigh more than its skeleton.

Breeding | Adults

AMERICAN WHITE PELICAN

Pelecanus erythrorhynchos L 62" (158 cm) W 108" (274 cm)

FIELD MARKS

Large, heavy waterbird

Massive bill and huge throat pocket

White with black primaries and outer secondaries

Breeding adult has yellow crest

Behavior

Due to large size, requires a lengthy running start. The American White Pelican is nevertheless a great flier, and flocks can be seen soaring high in the air or cruising low over water. Flocks travel in V-formation, wingbeats synchronized with the leader's. The American White Pelican does not dive from the air for its food but dips its bill into the water while swimming and corrals fish into its throat pouch.

Habitat

Prefers lakes, marshes, and salt bays, but breeds inland, nesting on small islands and feeding on shallow lakes, rivers, and marshes. Nests on the ground, but builds up a substantial mound that elevates the eggs, which are incubated on top of parents' webbed feet.

Local Sites

Can be sighted along most coastlines, but particularly on Sanibel Island at the J. N. "Ding" Darling National Wildlife Refuge.

FIELD NOTES During breeding season, the American White Pelican will forage at night, sometimes in groups that drive fish into shallower water where they are more easily scooped up. The cooperative hunting groups employ a wide range of strategies. Often pelicans must guard their catch against gulls that attempt to rob them of it.

Chick feeding | Adult *carolinensis*

BROWN PELICAN

Pelecanus occidentalis L 48" (122 cm) W 84" (213 cm)

FIELD MARKS

Smaller than American White Pelican, very long gray bill

Adult, gray-brown body and black belly; juvenile body is more brown

White head and neck with yellow wash; breeding adult's foreneck has yellow patch

Behavior

Dives from the air to capture its prey in surface water. Just before impact, its pouch balloons open, snatching small fish in its grasp. Some dives may be from as high as 60 feet in the air. Tilts its bill downward to drain water, tosses its head back to swallow. Sometimes gathers in large groups over transitory schools of fish, attracting other seabirds to the feeding frenzy. Flocks soar in long, staggered lines, alternately flapping and gliding in unison.

Habitat

Exclusively coastal, it makes its home along the immediate shoreline in sheltered bays, and near beaches. Breeds on islands in stick nests built from materials gathered or stolen by male for female.

Local Sites

Find the Brown Pelican in coastal areas and when traveling to Sanibel Island at the J. N. "Ding" Darling National Wildlife Refuge.

FIELD NOTES This smallest of the world's pelicans suffered a great decline in population during the mid-20th century due to the use of pesticides containing DDT. Disappeared completely for a time from Louisiana, the Pelican State. Has since made a significant recovery, and is now a common sight at the beach.

Immature | Juvenile

DOUBLE-CRESTED CORMORANT

Phalacrocorax auritus L 32" (81 cm) W 52" (132 cm)

FIELD MARKS
Large, rounded throat pouch is yellow-orange year-round

Bill is hooked at the tip

Breeding adult has a tuft of feathers curving behind eyes

Juvenile is brown with pale neck

Behavior
After locating prey at the surface, dives to considerable depths, propelling itself with legs and fully webbed feet. Uses its hooked bill to grasp fish. When it leaves the water, it perches on a dock or piling and half-spreads its wings to dry. Feeds on a variety of aquatic life and plants. May soar briefly at times, its neck in an S-shape. May swim, submerged to the neck.

Habitat
Common and widespread, the Double-crested Cormorant may be found along coasts, inland lakes, and rivers. The most numerous and far-ranging of North American cormorants, it adapts to fresh- or saltwater environments.

Local Sites
Some cormorants make Florida their year-round home, dispersing over short distances only. Many more inhabit Florida during breeding season and can also be seen in the extreme western Panhandle during their migration period.

FIELD NOTES The crests on the head of the breeding Double-crested Cormorant are rarely seen in the field. Eastern birds have black crests, less conspicuous than the white crests of those in the western part of its range.

Breeding | Adult male

ANHINGA

Anhinga anhinga L 35" (89 cm) W 45" (114 cm)

FIELD MARKS
Black with greenish sheen

Silvery-white spots and streaks
on wings and upper back

Females have buffy neck
and breast

Long, sharply pointed bill

Behavior
The Anhinga can control its buoyancy and often swims
with its body submerged and only its head above water.
Regularly dips its eyes below the surface as it hunts.
Spears fish with its long, sharp bill, then tosses them
into the air to catch and swallow. Often seen perched
on branches or stumps near water, wings outspread to
dry in the sun.

Habitat
Prefers freshwater ponds, lakes, cypress swamps,
and slow-moving rivers bordered by cypress trees
or mangroves. Range within the U.S. limited to subtropical regions of southern coasts. Wanderers venture
only a short distance north of breeding range.

Local Sites
A common resident of the peninsula, but rare in the
Keys and the Panhandle. In general, the Anhinga is
easy to find in any freshwater environment, including
Everglades National Park.

FIELD NOTES Flies with slow, regular wing beats and often soars
on rising thermal columns of air like a raptor. When soaring, it
holds its wings perpendicular to its body, forming a perfect cross
with its small head and long tail. It also spreads its tail in flight,
forming a fan.

Nonbreeding | Adult

GREAT BLUE HERON

Ardea herodias L 46" (117 cm) W 72" (183 cm)

FIELD MARKS

Large gray-blue heron

Black stripe extends above eye

White foreneck has black streaks

Breeding adult has yellowish bill
and ornate plumes on head

Juvenile has black crown

Behavior

Often seen standing or wading along calm shorelines
or rivers, foraging for food, or flying high, its head
folded back onto its shoulders. Emits an annoyed,
deep, guttural squawk as it takes flight. When threatened, draws its neck back with plumes erect and points
its bill at antagonist.

Habitat

May be seen hunting for aquatic creatures and,
occasionally, snakes and insects in marshes, shores, and
swamps. Beyond watery reaches, Great Blues can also
be found hunting mice and small woodchucks in farm
fields, meadows, and forest edges. Pairs of Great Blues
build large stick nests high up in trees, in loose associa-
tion with other Great Blue pairs. These "heronries" can
be located miles from water.

Local Sites

Common and widespread, the Great Blue is found
throughout Florida year-round. It may be easily
spotted in Everglades National Park and the Keys.

FIELD NOTES The all-white morph of this bird, found in southern
Florida, was once considered a species, called Great White
Heron. The offspring of a Great White and a Great Blue, called a
Wurdemann's Heron, is found primarily in the Keys.

Breeding | Adult

GREAT EGRET

Ardea alba L 39" (99 cm) W 51" (130 cm)

FIELD MARKS

Large white heron with a heavy yellow bill

Black legs and feet

Breeding adult has long plumes trailing from its back, extending beyond the tail

Behavior
Stalks its prey slowly and methodically, foraging in shallow water with sharply pointed bill to spear small fish, aquatic insects, frogs, and crayfish. Also known to hunt snakes, birds, and small mammals. May occasionally forage in groups or steal food from smaller birds.

Habitat
Common to both fresh- and saltwater wetlands, but also feeds in open fields. The Great Egret makes its nest in trees or shrubs 10 to 40 feet above the ground. Colonies may have a hundred birds. Occasionally breeds as far north as Canada.

Local Sites
Widespread across the state. Look especially for this bird afield in the J. N. "Ding" Darling Natural Wildlife Refuge near Fort Myers.

FIELD NOTES Early in the breeding season, the Great Egret grows long, ostentatious feathers called aigrettes from its scapulars. In the late 1800s, aigrettes were so sought after by the millinery industry that Great Egrets were hunted nearly to extinction. The grassroots campaign to end this trend later developed into the National Audubon Society. Today the loss of wetlands continues to threaten the Great Egret population.

Nonbreeding | Adult

SNOWY EGRET

Egretta thula L 24" (61 cm) W 41" (104 cm)

FIELD MARKS

White heron with slender black bill and legs, yellow eyes, lores, and feet

Breeding adult has upward-curving plumes on head, neck, and back; nonbreeding adult has shorter plumage

Behavior

An active feeder, the Snowy Egret may be seen running in shallows, chasing after its prey of fish, insects, and crustaceans. Also forages by stirring up bottom water with feet to flush out prey. In breeding display, the Snowy Egret raises all its plumage, pumping its head up and down and flashing the skin at the base of the bill, which turns from yellow to vermilion during breeding season. Also brays gutturally, pointing bill straight up.

Habitat

Prefers wetlands and sheltered bays along the coastline. Sedentary nesting populations are established in the subtropics and tropics during winter.

Local Sites

Widespread throughout the state year-round. Particularly large numbers of Snowy Egrets summer in Florida's western Panhandle.

FIELD NOTES The young Snowy Egret may be confused with the immature Little Blue Heron. The young Snowy Egret has a slimmer, mostly black bill, yellow lores, predominantly dark legs, and white wing tips, as opposed to the Little Blue Heron's two-toned bill with gray base and dark tip, mostly grayish lores, dull yellow legs and feet, and dusky wing tips.

Nonbreeding | Adult

LITTLE BLUE HERON

Egretta caerulea L 24" (61 cm) W 40" (102 cm)

FIELD MARKS

Slate blue; dull green legs, feet

Immature bird white with black wing tips; molts into adult plumage in first spring

Breeding adult has reddish-purple head and neck, black legs and feet

Behavior

A slow and methodical feeder that hunts for fish and small crustaceans. Away from the wetlands, it will also feed on insects such as grasshoppers. Strictly carnivorous, it depends on its sharply pointed bill to snag its prey. Like all herons, the Little Blue may be seen preening its contour and flight feathers with its pectinate, or comblike, middle toes.

Habitat

Prefers freshwater ponds, lakes, marshes, and coastal saltwater wetlands. After breeding, may disperse as far north as Newfoundland.

Local Sites

Common throughout most of Florida year-round. Get a good look at the Little Blue Heron on the boardwalk loop trail of the Corkscrew Swamp Sanctuary, just west of Imokalee.

FIELD NOTES The immature Little Blue Heron may be easily confused with the immature Snowy Egret until it acquires its characteristic slate-blue adult plumage. Also, the plumage of the male and female Little Blue Heron is identical, further complicating its identification in the field.

Nonbreeding | Adult

TRICOLORED HERON

Egretta tricolor L 26" (66 cm) W 36" (91 cm)

FIELD MARKS

Long, slender yellow bill with black tip; yellow legs

White belly and foreneck with dark blue upperparts

Brown patches at base of neck, lighter brown on lower back; immature has chestnut hindneck

Behavior

While foraging for food, sometimes stirs sediments from the bottom of water. Otherwise generally waits for prey to come near. Occasionally chases small fish, then uses its long, sharp beak to spear them. Prefers to forage for its food alone, and chases other birds away from its small hunting area. In flight, like other herons, the Tricolored draws its neck into an S-curve. Its neck has a sixth cervical vertebra, which allows quick, snakelike strikes while foraging.

Habitat

Common inhabitant of salt marshes and mangrove swamps on the eastern coastline and the Gulf Coast. Rarely found inland. Generally nests among a colony in trees, either on islands or near water.

Local Sites

Look for the Tricolored Heron year-round throughout Florida's marshes and swamps.

FIELD NOTES The Tricolored is the only member of the heron family to display countershading in its plumage: Its dark blue upperparts contrast sharply with its white belly and foreneck.

Breeding | Adult dark morphs

REDDISH EGRET

Egretta rufescens L 30" (76 cm) W 46" (117 cm)

FIELD MARKS
Pink bill with black tip

Breeding adult has shaggy
plumes on rufous head and neck

Breeding adult body and legs
cobalt blue

Immature gray, cinnamon markings

Behavior
While feeding, this heron lurches, dashing about with
wings flared, holding head and neck plumes on end.
Once it stops, it folds its wings over its head to form
a sort of canopy. Hunts for small fish by creating an
attractive shadow with its wings or by startling them
into the open.

Habitat
The Reddish Egret inhabits shallow, open salt pans and
mangrove swamps, preferring coastlines and islands.
Tends to stay along the Gulf Coast and the south Florida coast for the entire year, but may wander up the
Atlantic coast as far as New England. Does not migrate
extensively.

Local Sites
Look for this egret on Sanibel Island and along Florida's southern coastline.

FIELD NOTES The white morph of the Reddish Egret resembles
the immature Little Blue Heron or the Snowy Egret, but the
Reddish is larger in size and has a longer bill and dark legs.
Sometimes the dark morph of the Reddish Egret has considerable white on its wings and resembles a molting immature Little
Blue Heron. The Reddish is the only North American egret with
coloring other than white.

High Breeding | Adults

CATTLE EGRET

Bubulcus ibis L 20" (51 cm) W 36" (91 cm)

FIELD MARKS
Small, stocky, white heron with large, rounded head, yellow legs and bill

Throat feathering extends onto bill

Breeding adult has red-orange bill and orange-buff plumes on crown, back, and foreneck

Behavior
Often seen among livestock in fields, feeding on insects that have been flushed out by grazing cattle—hence the name. In the Cattle Egret's courtship ritual, a male aggressively establishes a territory and then is approached by a group of females, who bite his neck and back while he attempts to repel them. After three or four days, the male allows one of the females to stay. Mutual backbiting, stretching by the female, and twig-shaking by the male all occur, precursors to nest-building. Though silent for the most part, the Cattle Egret has been known to emit a two-tone *rick-rack* sound in nesting grounds.

Habitat
Widespread in open fields, on farms, in marshes, and even along highway edges. Nests in trees or shrubs, grouped in colonies. Wanders well north of breeding range, to the Canadian border.

Local Sites
Common throughout most of Florida. Migrates to South America in winter.

FIELD NOTES This Old World species came to South America from Africa, spread to Florida in the 1950s, reached California in the 1960s, and continues to expand its range today.

High Breeding | Adult male

GREEN HERON

Butorides virescens L 18" (46 cm) W 26" (66 cm)

FIELD MARKS

Small, chunky heron; short, dull yellow legs

Greenish-black crown feathers, sometimes a shaggy crest

Deep chestnut back, green and blue-gray upper, white center of throat and neck in adult

Behavior

Usually solitary, this heron's common cry of *kyowk* may be heard as it flies away. It stands at the edge of shallow water and tosses twigs, insects, even earthworms into the water as lures to attract minnows. The Green Heron spends most of its day in the shade. When alarmed, it may make a show by raising its crest, elongating its neck, flicking its tail, and in the process revealing its streaked throat plumage.

Habitat

Found in a variety of habitats but prefers streams, ponds, and marshes with woodland cover. Often perches in trees.

Local Sites

Generally common throughout the state. Look for this small loner particularly in the Everglades National Park.

FIELD NOTES Fossil specimens have indicated that the Green Heron hybridizes with the neotropical Striated Heron. This discovery prompted their being grouped into a single species, the Green-backed Heron. It was later determined that this mating was too infrequent to warrant the grouping, and in the 1990s, the two were resplit into seperate species, once again creating a niche for the Green Heron.

Breeding | Adult

YELLOW-CROWNED NIGHT-HERON

Nyctanassa violacea L 24" (61 cm) W 42" (107 cm)

FIELD MARKS
Stocky, short-necked heron with
gray-black bill, yellow legs

Adult has buffy-white crown,
black face, white cheeks, red
eyes; reddish legs when breeding

Juvenile is brownish-gray, slight
white spotting on upperparts

Behavior

The Yellow-crowned Night-Heron forages mainly at
night. A pickier eater than most herons, its short, broad
bill is adapted to its diet of insects, crabs, crayfish, and
mussels. It is known to forage for crabs in daytime
when feeding nestlings. A delayed emergence of crabs
in the spring will delay the Yellow-crowned's nesting
period. In flight, legs extend far beyond tail, head rests
on shoulders, and darker flight feathers and trailing
edge on wings show. Calls include a short *woc.*

Habitat

Roosts in trees in wet woods, swamps, mangroves,
bayous, and streams.

Local Sites

Look for this bird, uncommon but widespread in
Florida, in the Everglades National Park along the
Anhinga Trail.

FIELD NOTES A close relative, the Black-Crowned Night-Heron,
Nycticorax nycticorax, is white with black crown and back, a
white plume extending from the base of the neck, gray wings,
and yellow legs. The juvenile resembles that of the Yellow-
crowned, except browner and with bolder white spotting.

Year-round | Adult

WOOD STORK

Mycteria Americana L 40" (102 cm) W 61" (155 cm)

FIELD MARKS

Large, long-legged bird; white body, black flight feathers and tail, black legs and pink feet

Thick, dusky, downward-curving bill

Adult has bald, blackish gray head; juvenile has grayish brown head and yellow bill

Behavior

This endangered bird is the only stork native to North America. It wades through the water while foraging, swinging its submerged bill back and forth until prey approaches. Then it snaps its springlike bill shut in less than a tenth of a second. Often hunts in a group, herding and trapping prey. Feeds primarily on fish but also on other forms of aquatic life. Due to a weak, almost non-functional voice box, Wood Storks rattle their tongues and clack their bills to communicate.

Habitat

Prefers seasonally wet areas: cypress swamps, marshes, ponds, wet meadows, lagoons, and coastal shallows. Colonies nest in dense numbers in trees near pools with high concentrations of fish.

Local Sites

Look for the Wood Stork in the Cypress National Preserve, or southeast of Naples in the Conservancy Briggs Nature Center.

FIELD NOTES The Wood Stork flies with slow, deliberate beats of its long, broad wings, catching thermal air currents thousands of feet up. It can glide for miles with only an occasional flap of its wings. Watch for it soaring and circling like a hawk.

Year-round | Adult

WHITE IBIS

Eudocimus albus L 25" (64 cm) W 38" (97 cm)

FIELD MARKS

White plumage and pink facial
skin are distinctive

In breeding adult, facial skin, bill
and legs turn scarlet

Dark tips of primaries most easily
seen in flight

Behavior

Feeds in small groups, wading through shallow water
or marshland, thrusting its bill into soil to probe for
prey. Also sieves water for food with its bill. During
courtship, a mating pair rub their heads together, offer
grass and sticks to each other, and engage in mutual
preening. Gathers in dense colonies to build nests and
raise chicks.

Habitat

Abundant in coastal salt marshes, swamps, and mangroves. Also found in coastal lagoons and croplands
such as ricefields. Builds nests in trees or bushes, often
on islands offering protection against predation. Breeds
as far north as Virginia.

Local Sites

A year-round resident of the state, look for the White
Ibis among the Everglades or at Corkscrew Swamp
Sanctuary.

FIELD NOTES The Glossy Ibis, *Plegadis fal-
cinellus*, (inset) shares the same coastal
habitat as the White Ibis; both are currently
expanding north up the Atlantic seaboard.
The Glossy Ibis looks all black from a dis-
tance, but its chestnut plumage is glossed with green or purple.

Breeding | Adult

ROSEATE SPOONBILL

Ajaia ajaja L 32" (81 cm) W 50" (127 cm)

FIELD MARKS

Large wading bird with distinctive long spatulate bill

Unfeathered greenish head, may become buffy during courtship

Pink body with scarlet fringing on wings and rump

Behavior

Often seen in a small group, swinging its head from side to side, sweeping its long, flat, sensitive, partially open bill through shallow water as it feeds on small fish and invertebrates. When food sources are scarce, the Roseate Spoonbill resorts to seeds and insects. Courting pairs rub heads together, offer grass and sticks to each other, and engage in mutual preening.

Habitat

Prefers shallow salt- and freshwater marshes and lagoons and mangrove-bordered saltwater flats Often nests in colonies on close strings of islands, a setting that offers protection against predators.

Local Sites

Fairly common along both coasts and throughout the Keys. Casual appearances north to the mid-Atlantic coast and at inland lakes and marshes. Year-round resident of Sanibel Island; regular visitor to Everglades National Park.

FIELD NOTES From a distance, the Roseate Spoonbill can look like the Greater Flamingo, *Phoenicopterus ruber* (inset), but the bulky, angled, black-tipped bill of the flamingo immediately distinguishes it.

Year-round | Adult

TURKEY VULTURE

Cathartes aura L 27" (67 cm) W 69" (175 cm)

FIELD MARKS
Naked red head, ivory bill,
red legs

Brownish black feathers over
body, silver-gray flight feathers

In flight, contrasting underwings
show and long tail extends
beyond feet

Behavior
An excellent flier, the Turkey Vulture soars high above
the ground in search of carrion and refuse, watching
for other scavengers. Rocks from side to side in flight,
seldom flapping its wings, which are held upward in a
shallow V, allowing it to gain lift from conditions that
would deter any other raptor. Feeds heavily when food
is available but can go days without if necessary.

Habitat
Hunts in open country, woodlands, and farms, even
at urban dumps and landfills. Nests solitarily in
hollow logs or, less frequently, in hollow trees, crevices,
caves, and mine shafts. Expansion of Turkey Vultures
in the Northeast is considered a result of increased
numbers of White-tailed Deer and, consequently,
increased roadkill.

Local Sites
Common throughout Florida. Some Turkey Vultures
will migrate long distances, even to South America.

FIELD NOTES The Turkey Vulture's naked head is an adaptation
that keeps it from soiling its feathers while feeding and reduces
the risk of picking up disease from carcasses. It also has an
unusually well-developed sense of smell, allowing it to locate
carrion concealed in forest settings.

Year-round | Adult

BLACK VULTURE

Coragyps atratus L 25" (64 cm) W 57" (145 cm)

FIELD MARKS
Small, unfeathered head and hooked bill

Sooty, black plumage

Shows large white patches at base of primaries in flight

White legs, gray-white feet

Behavior
Soars to great heights, flapping its wings rapidly and gliding for short distances on flattened wings in between. Feeds primarily on carrion and refuse, for which its unfeathered head is adapted, but is also known to occasionally feed on live prey, eating it alive rather than killing it first as hawks do. Can go many days without food if necessary. Does not build a nest, rather both male and female incubate eggs carefully and attend to young for months after fledging.

Habitat
Common in open country and near human settlements, where they scavenge in garbage dumps. Breeds often in dark recesses of abandoned buildings or under the cover of caves or hollow trunks.

Local Sites
See it roosting early in the morning with wings spread to catch the ultraviolet rays of the sun year-round across the state, particularly along the Gulf Coast.

FIELD NOTES Not quite as adept at spotting carrion and without a keen sense of smell, the Black Vulture will compensate with particularly aggressive behavior at feed sites, often harping on a Turkey Vulture's find and claiming it as its own.

Immature | Juvenile female

OSPREY

Pandion haliaetus L 22-25" (56-64 cm) W 58-72" (147-183 cm)

FIELD MARKS

Dark brown above, white below

White head, with prominent dark eye stripe

Gray beak

Females have darker streaking on neck

Behavior

Hunts by soaring over water, hovering, then diving down and plunging feet first into water to snatch its prey with specialized barbs on its toes. Feeds only on fish. Call is a series of clear, resonant, whistled *kyew*s, which herald the arrival of spring for Atlantic coast residents. The Osprey also uses its call during breeding to draw a female's attention to a prized fish hooked in its talons.

Habitat

Vacates the United States after breeding season yet returns early from wintering grounds in Central and South America. Nests near bodies of fresh- or saltwater. Its large, bulky nests are built up in trees or on sheds, poles, docks, or specialized man-made platforms. Uncommon inland yet found on all continents except Antarctica.

Local Sites

Common throughout the state. Look for Osprey in the Florida Keys, particularly Key Largo, and in south-eastern Florida near Hobe Sound.

FIELD NOTES Females tend to be larger than males—an advantage for eggs, as females do the majority of brooding, and for hatchlings, as a greater variety of food is thus made available.

Year-round | Adult

SWALLOW-TAILED KITE

Elanoides forficatus L 23" (58 cm) W 48" (122 cm)

FIELD MARKS

Long, deeply forked black tail;
juveniles have shorter tail

Striking, sharply defined pattern
of black and white

In flight, silhouette is similar to
young Magnificent Frigatebird

Behavior

The Swallow-tailed Kite is one of the most agile and
graceful fliers in the world of birds. Aloft for many
hours at a time, it deftly snatches flying insects, especially dragonflies. It also preys upon snakes, lizards,
and young birds, often eating in flight. It also drinks
in flight, skimming the water like a swallow. Social to
an extent, several kites may be seen hunting together,
but even more gather in large, communal roosts in
late summer before their winter migration to Central
and South America.

Habitat

Found in open woods, bottomlands, and wetlands.
Nests in the tops of tall trees.

Local Sites

Fairly common spring through summer in Florida's
central and southern peninsula and the Keys. Often
seen in Everglades National Park. Vacates North
America after breeding season, wintering to the South.

FIELD NOTES The Swallow-tailed, like other kites, lacks the bony
ridge over the eye exhibited by all other hawks. This lends it an
almost benign appearance in contrast to the brooding look of the
Bald or Golden Eagle.

Year-round | Adult

WHITE-TAILED KITE

Elanus leucurus L 16" (41 cm) W 42" (107 cm)

FIELD MARKS
Long, pointed wings

Black shoulder patches show as
black leading edges in flight

Long, mostly white tail and white
underparts; juvenile head and
underparts lightly streaked rufous,
which quickly fades

Behavior
Hovers while hunting with tail down and limbs
dangling, hanging motionless in the wind like its
namesake but unlike any other North American kite.
Swoops to clutch prey in its strong talons. Feeds
primarily on rodents and insects but, not a picky eater,
takes advantage of opportunities to snatch other prey.
Call is a brief, whistled *keep keep keep.*

Habitat
Fairly common year-round in grasslands, farmlands,
cultivated fields, and even highway median strips. Also
makes its home in river valleys and marshes. Forms
winter roosts of over a hundred birds.

Local Sites
Look for the White-tailed Kite around Lake Okeechobee and environs.

FIELD NOTES The Mississippi Kite, *Ictinia mississippiensis*
(inset), is similar but distinguished by a black tail and
gray underparts. It also lacks the black shoulders of
the White-tailed Kite, previously known as the
Black-shouldered Kite. The juvenile Mississippi
is heavily streaked and spotted, with pale
bands on the tail. It may be found in the
Panhandle area of Florida.

Year-round | Adult female

SNAIL KITE

Rostrhamus sociabilis L 17" (43 cm) W 46" (117 cm)

FIELD MARKS
Paddle-shaped wings

Thin, deeply hooked bill

Male gray-black with white
uppertail and undertail coverts

Female dark brown with
distinctive head pattern

Behavior
Chief and only food is apple snail, for which it hunts
slowly over marshlands, with considerable flapping of
wings, and with head and bill held down. Snatches
snail with talons, then flies it to perch. Distinctive bill
is specially adapted to reach into apple snail's shell and
remove the soft body of the large gastropod. Courtship
flight consists of repeated soars and dives with wings
folded. Listen for call of *kor-ee-ee-a koree-a*.

Habitat
Subtropical freshwater marshes of Southern Florida,
wherever one might find the apple snail. Roosts in
groups on low bushes over water. Nests alone or in
loose colonies in low tree or hammock of marsh grass.

Local Sites
Look for this endangered species just northwest of
Boca Raton at the Arthur R. Marshall Loxahatchee
National Wildlife Refuge and in the Northern section
of the Everglades at Shark Valley Visitor Center.

FIELD NOTES The Snail Kite's ability to find its food is greatly
affected by shifting water levels, so the bird wanders widely in
search of favorable feeding conditions. Once reduced to only
a few remaining pairs, the Snail Kite has made something of a
comeback, yet remains on the endangered species list.

Year-round | Adult male

Circus cyaneus L 17-23" (43-58 cm) W 38-48" (97-122 cm)

FIELD MARKS
Owl-like facial disk

Slim body; long, narrow wings
with rounded tips; long tail

Adult male gray above, whitish
below; female brown above,
whitish below, with brown streaks
on breast and flanks

Behavior
Harriers generally perch low and fly close to the
ground, wings upraised, as they search for birds, mice,
frogs, and other prey. They seldom soar high except
during migration and in exuberant, acrobatic courtship
display, during which the male loops and somersaults
in the air. Often found hunting in the dim of dawn or
dusk, using their well-developed hearing made possible
by hidden ears. Identifiable by a thin, insistent whistle.

Habitat
Commonly called the Marsh Hawk, this harrier can
often be found in wetlands and open country. Nests
invariably on the ground. During winter, roosts comu-
nally on the ground, alongside the Short-eared Owl.

Local Sites
Find the Northern Harrier in Everglades National Park
during the winter months.

FIELD NOTES Careful when attempting to identify a Northern
Harrier high overhead. It can look like a falcon when gliding, due
to its long, broad tail, or like an accipiter when soaring, due to
the rounded tips of its wings. Look for its bright white rump,
though, one of the most noticeable field marks of any hawk.

Year-round | Adult

BALD EAGLE

Haliaeetus leucocephalus L 31-37" (79-94 cm) W 70-90" (178-229 cm)

FIELD MARKS

Distinctive white head and tail

Large yellow beak, feet, and eyes

Brown body

Juveniles mostly dark, showing
blotchy white on underwing
and tail

Behavior

Rock-steady fliers, rarely swerving or tipping on their
flattened wings as Turkey Vultures do. Bald Eagles feed
mainly on fish, but often on carrion and injured squirrels, rabbits, and muskrats as well. Sometimes steal fish
from other birds of prey. They lock talons and cart-
wheel together through the sky in an elaborate dance
during courtship.

Habitat

A member of the sea eagle group, most often lives and
feeds along seacoasts or along rivers and lakes. Known
to perch on tall trees or on sandbars of rivers rich in
salmon. Will also be spotted in Florida swamps. The
Bald Eagle will nest solitarily in tall trees or on cliffs.

Local Sites

Found year-round throughout Florida, the Bald Eagle
can be viewed during breeding season in southeastern
Florida at the Jonathan Dickinson State Park. Also
known to begin breeding as early as November at St.
Marks National Wildlife Refuge on the Panhandle.

FIELD NOTES The Bald Eagle's nest is characterized by a
collection of sticks lined with finer materials, high in a tree or in a
cliff's crevice. Making great strides in recovery after pesticide
bans, the Bald Eagle population is most abundant in Alaska, and
has been moved from endangered to threatened status.

Immature | Juvenile

SHARP-SHINNED HAWK

Accipiter striatus L 10-14" (25-36 cm) W 20-28" (51-71 cm)

FIELD MARKS

Squared-off tail with narrow white tip

Long, thin, yellow legs

Smallish head; streaks on head
blend into back

In flight, wings appear to bend
back as if at wrists

Behavior

Preys chiefly on small birds, often engaging in ambush
maneuvers or aggressive pursuit even through thick
foliage and undergrowth. Flight consists of several
quick wing beats and a glide, its maneuvers assisted by
a long, rudderlike tail.

Habitat

Found for the most part in mixed woodlands, though
can be seen in the open air, mostly during migration
periods in spring and fall. Nests are substantial stick
structures constructed in tall trees.

Local Sites

At the Dry Tortugas National Park, 70 miles west of
Key West, look for the Sharp-shinned Hawk on the
prowl for food during its spring migration.

FIELD NOTES The Sharp-shinned is easily
confused with its relative, the Cooper's
Hawk, *Accipiter cooperii* (inset). The
Cooper's is larger with a longer, more
rounded tail and a larger, light-colored
head. The aggressive nature of accipiters
is shown in the story of a farmer who
shooed her chicken from the yard into the kitchen
to protect it from a Cooper's. The hawk flew through the
screen door and took the chicken anyway!

Year-round | Adult

RED-SHOULDERED HAWK

Buteo lineatus L 15"-19" (38cm-48 cm) W 37"-42" (94cm-107 cm)

FIELD MARKS

Long-tailed and long-legged

Pale white to cream beak with black tip

Adult has reddish shoulders, wing linings, chest with white striping

Brown above with white spotting

Behavior

The Red-shouldered Hawk flies with slow wing beats. Hunts from low perches, trees, posts, and utility poles, for small mammals such as rabbits, squirrels, rats, mice, and voles. Call is an evenly spaced series of clear, high *kee-ah* or *kah* notes. Look for the juvenile, with coloring that is more finely striped white and brown than the adult's.

Habitat

Prefers woodlands, especially moist, mixed woods near water and swamps. Nests along the trunks of trees about 10-200 feet up. Known to retain the same territory for years, sometimes even passing it down to succeeding generations.

Local Sites

Look for the Red-shouldered Hawk throughout the state. Good sites for spotting these raptors include the Everglades National Park and Big Cypress National Preserve at the tip of the peninsula, as well as south-east of Sarasota in the Myakka River State Park.

FIELD NOTES In south Florida, keep watch for the smallest and palest race of the Red-shouldered species, the *Buteo lineatus extimus*, with barred, light rufous underparts, reddish wing linings, and a long, black tail with narrow white bands.

Year-round | Adult rufous morph *calurus*

RED-TAILED HAWK

Buteo jamaicensis L 22" (56 cm) W 50" (127 cm)

FIELD MARKS
Brown body, heavy beak

Variable pale and dark feathers on
mantle, forming a broad "V"

Distinctive red tail

Whitish belly with dark streaks

Dark bar on edge of underwing

Behavior
Watch the Red-tailed Hawk hover in place, searching
for prey, sometimes kiting, or hanging motionless in
the wind, in its search for food. Will partially eat large
prey on the ground, but more often carries small prey
back to perch. Listen for its distinctive call, a harsh,
descending *keeeeer*. Preys on rodents. Juveniles are
heavily brown with brown streaks and spots below and
gray-brown tails.

Habitat
Found in more habitats than any other North American *buteo*, from woods with nearby open lands to
plains, prairie groves, and even deserts. Scan for hawks
along habitat edges, where field meets forest or wetlands meet woodlands. Red-tailed Hawks favor these
areas because of the variety of prey found there.

Local Sites
Common throughout Florida year-round, but look for
extraordinarily large gatherings of these hawks in the
southern part of the state.

FIELD NOTES The gregarious Red-tailed Hawk will usually
migrate in large flocks, sometimes with other hawk species.
This hawk can soar at altitudes of up to 5,000 feet, appearing
more often than not as a speck against a clear sky. Use your
binoculars to sight them against the clouds.

Year-round | Adult

CRESTED CARACARA

Caracara cheriway L 23" (58 cm) W 50" (127 cm)

FIELD MARKS

Blackish-brown overall, with white throat and neck

Large head, long neck, long legs

Red-orange to yellow facial skin

Shows whitish patch near end of rounded wings

Behavior

Soars with broad, flapping wings held flat and fanned tail much like a raven. Forages on the ground in search of food, often in the company of vultures. Feeds on carrion, and also large insects, reptiles, small mammals, birds, and fish. Sometimes known to kill live prey such as nestling birds. Though usually silent, calls include a low rattle and a single *wuck* note. As in all falcons, females are larger than males and juveniles are easily distinguished. The juvenile Caracara is browner, upperparts edged and spotted with buff, underparts streaked with buff.

Habitat

Inhabits open brushlands.

Local Sites

Southern Florida is one of the only places in the U.S. to see the Crested Caracara. Look for it scavenging on roadkilled armadillos around Lake Okeechobee, especially along Fla. 70 east of Arcadia, County Road 74 east of Babcock, or the part of US 27 connecting them.

FIELD NOTES The Crested Caracara is the only member of the family Falconidae that goes to the trouble of building a nest. It does this fifteen to thirty feet up in palmetto trees or giant cacti, and it is built by both the male and female out of sticks, vines, and twigs.

Year-round | Adult male

Falco sparverius L 10½" (27 cm) W 23" (58 cm)

HAWKS, FALCONS

FIELD MARKS

Russet back and tail

Double black stripes on white face

Male has blue-gray wing coverts and shows a distinctive row of white circular spots on trailing edge of wing

Behavior

Feeds on insects, reptiles, mice, and other small mammals, often hovering over prey before plunging. Will also feed on small birds, especially in winter. Regularly seen perched on telephone lines and fenceposts, frequently bobbing its tail. Has a clear call of *killy killy killy.*

Habitat

The most widely distributed falcon, it is commonly seen in open country and in cities, often mousing in highway medians or sweeping down the surf line. Nests in tree holes and often in barns using little to no nesting material. A pair nesting in the eaves of one's barn is considered a fortunate sign.

Local Sites

Common throughout Florida, the American Kestrel is a year-round resident throughout the state except the western tip of the Panhandle, where it winters.

FIELD NOTES Related to the Kestrel, the Peregrine Falcon, *Falco peregrinus* (inset), sports a distinctive black helmet, rufous breast spotted with brown, and white and brown legs and tail. Feeds on birds and is often seen in cities. Look for it as well on Garden Key at Dry Tortugas National Park.

Year-round | Adult

LIMPKIN

Aramus guarauna L 26" (66 cm)

FIELD MARKS
Chocolate brown overall

Densely streaked with white

Long, slightly downcurved bill

Long legs and large, webless, dull
grayish green feet

Juvenile paler than adult

Behavior
Named for its unusual limping gait, commonly wades
or swims in search of snails, frogs, crustaceans, and
insects. Uses its long bill as a probe to catch food in
mud or water by sight and touch. Its eerie, piercing
calls of *krr-oww* can be heard chiefly at night, delivered
by both male and female.

Habitat
Found predominantly in the swamps and marshy wetlands where its chief prey, large apple snails, are found
in abundance.

Local Sites
Predominantly found in central Florida, a casual visitor
to southeastern Georgia as well. The two-mile boardwalk loop of Corkscrew Swamp Sanctuary, west of
Immokalee, is a prime area to see the Limpkin
feeding on apple snails, as is the Edward Ball Wakulla
Springs State Park, which includes the largest and
deepest freshwater spring in the world.

FIELD NOTES The Limpkin is the last remaining member of the
once widespread Aramidae family. Hunted to near extirpation
in Florida in the early 1900s, its population has increased and
stabilized due to federal laws and established sanctuaries, yet
it is still threatened by the draining and degradation of wetlands
due to atmospheric and man-made conditions.

Breeding | Adult

COMMON MOORHEN

Gallinula chloropus L 14" (36 cm)

FIELD MARKS
Red bill with yellow tip

Red forehead shield, black head
and neck

Brownish olive back, slate
underparts

White streak on flanks

Behavior
Feeds on a variety of plant matter and invertebrates,
but occasionally eats amphibians, small reptiles, and
even carrion. Long yellow legs, marked by a reddish
band at the top, allow these birds to wade easily. Common Moorhen take food from exposed mud or the
water's surface. They will sometimes swim while foraging. Look for the juvenile, which is paler brown with
white throat and dusky bill and legs.

Habitat
Prefers freshwater marshes, ponds, and placid rivers.
Nests in marshlands, establishing open, floating nests.

Local Sites
Common throughout the state. Pay close attention to
marsh margins in St. Marks National
Wildlife Reserve.

FIELD NOTES Common Moorhen is
distinguished at all ages from Purple Gallinule, *Porphyrula
martinica* (inset), by a white side stripe. The Purple Gallinule has
a red bill tipped in yellow, but the forehead shield is pale blue,
and the head, neck, and underparts are bright purplish-blue.

Year-round | Adults

AMERICAN COOT

Fulica americana L 15½" (39 cm)

FIELD MARKS

Blackish head and neck

Small, reddish-brown forehead

Whitish bill with dark band at tip

Slate body

Outer feathers of undertail coverts white, inner black

Behavior

The distinctive toes of the American Coot are flexible and lobed, permitting them to swim well in open water and even dive in pursuit of aquatic vegetation beneath the surface. They are the only rails with the ability to dive and stay submerged to feed. They bob their small heads back and forth when walking or swimming and may be seen foraging in large flocks, especially during the winter. Note leg color, which ranges from green in juveniles to yellow in adults.

Habitat

Nests in freshwater marshes, in wetlands, or near lakes and ponds. Winters in both fresh and salt water. Has also adapted well to human-altered habitats including pits and sewage lagoons for foraging, or suburban lawns for resting.

Local Sites

Common to abundant throughout Florida. As it is the most widespread species of rail, it is often the most easily observed.

FIELD NOTES The American Coot, like the Common Moorhen, will build a floating nest, made of dead stems, lined with other material, and anchored to aquatic vegetation, in which it will generally lay six eggs each year.

Year-round | Adult *crepitans*

CLAPPER RAIL

Rallus Longirostris L 14½" (37 cm)

FIELD MARKS
Plumage variable, but always grayish edges on brown-centered back feathers, olive wing coverts

Short, rounded wings

Short tail

Long, thin bill

Behavior
Uses long, thin bill to probe into subsurface crevices and holes, such as those of fiddler crabs. Generally a solitary forager, but may be seen feeding with a mate or young during breeding season. Its distinctive call is an accelerating, then slowing, crescendo of ten or more *kek kek kek* notes, employed when seeking a mate and when migrating.

Habitat
Coastal salt marshes. Nests are deeply concealed and constructed of marsh vegetation.

Local Sites
Look for the Clapper Rail along the edges of wetlands at Merritt Island National Wildlife Refuge, adjacent to the Kennedy Space Center, or on canals that cut through salt marshes along the entire east coast. Clapper Rails are less likely found on the west coast, where populations have declined because of the introduction of the red fox.

FIELD NOTES Even where they are abundant, Clapper Rails can be extremely difficult to see well. Making a sharp, repeated clucking or clapping sound with one's mouth may be enough to lure a male into the open at the edge of a salt marsh. The best time to try this is early during the breeding season, from April through June.

Year-round | Adult with chicks

SANDHILL CRANE

Grus canadensis L 34-48" (86-122 cm) W 73-90" (185-229 cm)

FIELD MARKS
Plumage is gray overall

Dull red skin on crown and lores

Whitish chin, cheek, and upper
throat

Black primaries

Juvenile lacks red patch

Behavior
Stands with body horizontal, picking grain, seed, fruit,
insects, and small vertebrates from surface of wetlands
or farm fields. Call is a loud, trumpeting *gar-oo-oo*,
delivered frequently and intensely during courtship
displays. Courtship consists of standardized move-
ments of head, neck, and wings, paired with frenzied
leaps resembling ballet moves. Preens itself with a
muddy bill, staining the feathers of the upper back,
lower neck, and breast.

Habitat
Breeds on tundra, grasslands, and in marshes, building
mounds of moist vegetation for nests. In winter,
regularly feeds in dry fields, returning to water at night.

Local Sites
Residents and winterers alike abound
at the Paynes Prairie State Preserve,
ten miles south of Gainesville.

FIELD NOTES The Whooping Crane, *Grus
americana* (inset), is white overall with black
primaries that show in flight and a red crimson crown similar
to that of the related Sandhill. An endangered species, it often
accompanies the Sandhill during migration. A small population
has also been introduced into Florida.

Breeding | Adult male

BLACK-BELLIED PLOVER

Pluvialis squatarola L 11½" (29 cm)

FIELD MARKS
Roundish heads and bodies, large
eyes, short bills, dark legs

Mottled gray, white belly in winter
and juveniles

Breeding male has frosted cap,
black and white spots on back
and wings, black bill

Behavior
Hunts in small, loose groups for invertebrates and
small mollusks such as worms, shrimp, insects, eggs,
and small crabs. Sometimes eats berries. Plovers locate
their prey by sight, darting across the ground, stopping,
then running off again. When they do fly, they can be
identified by a barred tail and a black patch where the
wing attaches to the body.

Habitat
Shorebird that prefers sandy shores and beaches, so
rare in interior regions. Nests on the Arctic tundra.

Local Sites
Found occasionally throughout the state during fall
migration from late July to September. The Black-
bellied Plover winters along the entire coastline of
Florida, especially along the Gulf Coast.

FIELD NOTES Listen for the Black-bellied Plover's drawn-out,
three-note whistle, the second note lower-pitched than the
others. Note that the juveniles of this species may be gold-
speckled above.

Breeding | Adult male

WILSON'S PLOVER

Charadrius wilsonia L 7¾" (20 cm)

FIELD MARKS

Long, heavy, black bill

Broad neck band, black in breeding male, brown in female and winter male

Grayish pink legs

Juvenile resembles adult female

Behavior

Runs short distances, then stops with upright posture and head held high, looking for moving prey with its large eyes. Sometimes stamps feet alternately, causing prey to rise to ground surface. Seizes worms, small mollusks, shrimp, insects, small crabs, or larvae by pecking. Drinks by lowering its bill horizontal to water's surface. Flies swiftly on long, pointed wings. Call is a sharp, whistled *whit*.

Habitat

Fairly common but declining on barrier islands, sandy beaches, and mudflats near river mouths or inlets. Nests above high-tide line in simple scrapes or depressions in beach areas.

Local Sites

Look for Wilson's Plover year-round on the beaches of the peninsula and in spring and summer nesting season along the St. Marks National Wildlife Refuge shore. The J. N. "Ding" Darling National Wildlife Refuge on Sanibel Island is also home to many.

FIELD NOTES If the nest of a Wilson's Plover is threatened, the female will scuttle about, scraping other nests in an attempt to distract the trespasser. A crippled bird act is also often employed to divert attention away from a nest.

Year-round | Adult

KILLDEER

Charadrius vociferus L 10½" (27 cm)

FIELD MARKS

Tan to chocolate brown above, white neck and belly

Black double breast bands

Black stripe on forehead and extending back from black bill

Reddish eye ring

Behavior

Well-known for feigning a broken wing when predators come near its nest, it will limp to one side, drag its wing, and spread its tail. Once intruders are away from the nest, the instantly healed Killdeer will take flight and can then be identified by its reddish-orange rump. Often seen running, then stopping on a dime with an inquisitive look, then suddenly jabbing at the ground with its bill. May gather in loose flocks. Feeds mainly on insects that live in short vegetation.

Habitat

Although a type of plover, the Killdeer generally prefers interior grassy regions, but may also be found on shores. In summer, it can be found across the entire continent of North America south of the tundra. Builds nest on open ground, usually on gravel.

Local Sites

Common throughout Florida year-round, and may be found in fallow fields, city parking lots, golf courses, and other areas in close proximity to humans.

FIELD NOTES The Killdeer's loud, piercing, eponymous call of *kill-dee* or its ascending *dee-dee-dee* is often the signal for identifying these birds before sighting them. Listen also for a long, trilled *trrrrrrr* during courtship displays or when a nest is threatened by a predator.

Year-round | Adult

AMERICAN OYSTERCATCHER

Haematopus palliatus L 18½" (47 cm)

FIELD MARKS

Large, red-orange bill

Black head, dark brown back

White wing, tail patches, and underparts

Juvenile is scaly-looking above, with dark tip on bill for first year

Behavior

Feeds in shallow water among a small, noisy flock, using its chisel-shaped bill to crack an opening in the shells of clams, oysters, and mussels. Then severs the shellfish's constrictor muscle and pries the shell open. Also probes sand and mud for worms and crabs. Calls are vocal and variable, including a piercing, repeated whistle; a loud, piping call; and a single loud whistle. Courtship consists of calls coupled with ritualized flights of shallow, rapid wing beats and displays of side-by-side running or rotating in place.

Habitat

Coastal beaches, mudflats, and rocky outcroppings. Nests in a scrape or bowl-shaped depression in sand, in grass, on rock, or on gravel or shells piled above the high-tide line.

Local Sites

Seen and heard year-round along the Gulf and Atlantic Coasts at low tide, and along the way from the mainland to Sanibel Island.

FIELD NOTES There are several good commercial recordings available of the American Oystercatcher, a useful tool, since their calls are as distinctive as their bills—and even more noticeable.

Breeding | Adult

AMERICAN AVOCET

Recurvirostra americana L 18" (46 cm)

FIELD MARKS
Black and white with white belly

Long, bluish legs and feet

Sharply recurved bill, longer and
straighter in males

Rusty head and neck plumage in
breeding adult

Behavior
Feeds with a flock in shallow water by walking in a
loose line of sometimes 100 birds, sweeping its slightly
open bill in a scything motion through the water, lightly brushing the bottom for fish and invertebrates. In
deeper water, may feed by tipping over, much like a
dabbling duck. The birds will also feed on insect larvae,
small crustaceans, and other invertebrates. Only avocet
to have distinct winter and breeding plumage; gray
head and neck in winter, rusty cinnamon in summer.
Call is a loud *wheet* or *pleeet*.

Habitat
A graceful wader that prefers coastal areas, alkaline
lakes, and briney ponds for foraging. The American
Avocet is very tolerant of cold and will winter as far
north as the Outer Banks of North Carolina, even in icy
conditions. Nests on flat ground or on a marsh near
water in construction of dry grasses and mud.

Local Sites
Look for the American Avocet during the winter
months along the Atlantic coastline of Florida.

FIELD NOTES The American Avocet's bill is so sensitive that it
defends itself against intruders with its wings and feet rather
than with its pointed bill. This species is currently on an upswing
after overhunting in the 19th and 20th centuries.

Year-round | Adult male

BLACK-NECKED STILT

Himantopus mexicanus L 14" (36 cm)

FIELD MARKS

Glossy black, needle-thin bill

White underparts, white around eyes

Long red-orange legs

Males dark black from head, down
back, to tail; female and juveniles
dark brown

Behavior

Tall and elegant, the Black-necked Stilt feeds quietly
in small flocks. Disturbed, the flock transforms into
a flailing, chaotic mob, splashing water and whistling
wildly on take-off, sometimes even attacking intruders.
Hunts for insects and worms by walking rapidly along
the shore, and for small fish, shrimp, and frogs by
wading into waters deeper than those chosen by other
shorebirds. May be seen alone, in pairs, or in small
flocks. Call is a loud *kek kek kek*.

Habitat

Breeds and winters in a wide variety of wet habitats
but partial to fresh water. Nests on the ground in
loose colonies hidden by grasses in Arctic or subarctic
regions. These stilts are monogamous and beginning
at about three years old tend clutches of four eggs each
year in nests of sticks, grasses, rocks, and fish bones.

Local Sites

Look for Black-necked Stilts nesting around Myakka
River State Park east of Sarasota.

FIELD NOTES A warm-weather bird, it resides year-round
throughout the peninsula. This stilt is easily recognized by its
red-orange legs, which, at eight to ten inches long, are some of
the longest proportionally of any birds.

Nonbreeding | Adult

LESSER YELLOWLEGS

Tringa flavipes L 10½" (27 cm)

FIELD MARKS

Long yellow legs, rarely orange

Dark, thin, straight bill

Breeding plumage shows finely streaked breast and fine, short bars on flanks

Winter plumage paler overall

Behavior

Bobs and teeters actively in a high-stepping gait while feeding, using its spikey bill to capture small fish or to probe in mud for worms, insects, and small crustaceans. Especially loud and vocal, its call is a series of high, short *tew* notes. If flushed, the Yellowleg will sound off, warning other shorebirds of the perceived danger. If a nest is threatened, it hounds the trespasser vocally without let-up.

Habitat

Nests noisily on sub-Arctic tundra or woodland, preferring raised piles of leaves or vegetation near the water. Most Lesser Yellowlegs winter in South America, but some winter in the United States.

Local Sites

A regular summer visitor to coastal Florida, look for the Lesser Yellowlegs during a falling tide, when the prospect for fresh food is high.

FIELD NOTES At 14" (36 cm), the Greater Yellowlegs, *Tringa melanoleuca* (inset), is larger, with a longer, stouter, and often slightly upturned bill. It is more heavily barred and faintly two-toned in winter. It is also distinguished from the Lesser Yellowlegs by its voice and its descending call.

Breeding | Adult *semipalmatus*

WILLET

Catoptrophorus semipalmatus L 15" (38 cm)

FIELD MARKS
Large, plump, with long gray legs

Breeding adult is heavily mottled; white belly

Winter plumage pale gray above

In flight, shows black and white wing pattern with black edges

Behavior
The Willet, like other shorebirds, wades through the water in search of prey, probing through mud with its long bill. Feeds primarily on aquatic insects and their larvae. Forages on land for seeds and rice as well. Its call of *pill-will-willet*, heard commonly on breeding grounds, is the genesis of its name, but it may also be heard giving a *kip-kip-kip* call when alarmed. As protective as they are, parents are known to leave unhatched eggs behind once the first young leaves the nest. Sleeps on one leg with head tucked in on its back.

Habitat
Nests in wetlands during the spring and summer months, usually within 200 feet of another Willet nest. Moves more toward the coastline in winter. Look for the juvenile, which is mottled golden brown.

Local Sites
Found year-round along the coastline of the northern two-thirds of the state. In winter, look for the Willet perched high on a rock or post around the coastal beaches of south Florida and the Keys.

FIELD NOTES During courtship displays, the Willet will show its black and white underwing patches, one of the more identifiable fieldmarks of this otherwise fairly nondescript bird. Keep an eye out as well for the white tail and rump.

Breeding | Adult male

RUDDY TURNSTONE

Arenaria interpres L 9½" (24 cm)

FIELD MARKS
Stout bird with short bill and legs

Orange legs and feet

Breeding adult has striking black
and white head and bib, black
and chestnut back

Adult female is duller than male

Behavior
The Ruddy Turnstone uses its slender bill to flip aside
shells and pebbles in search of aquatic insects, small
fish, mollusks, crustaceans, worms, and eggs. Its
distinctive call sounds like a low, guttural rattle.

Habitat
Makes its nest on the ground in coastal tundra or freshwater areas and migrates to milder, saltwater tidal areas
for the winter, taking advantage of the greater availability of invertebrates found there.

Local Sites
May be seen sporadically throughout Florida during
fall migration, but is more readily found along the
coastline during winter months, when the bird can be
identified by its back, head, and wing color, which
turns from black to brown.

FIELD NOTES In flight, the Ruddy Turnstone's complex pattern on
back and wings makes it easily identifiable.

Breeding | Adult

SANDERLING

Calidris alba L 8" (20 cm)

FIELD MARKS

In winter, pale gray above, white below

Bill and legs black

Prominent white wing stripe

Rusty head, mantle, and breast plumage during breeding

Behavior

Feeds on sandy beaches, chasing retreating waves in order to snatch up newly exposed mollusks and crustaceans, then darts to avoid the oncoming surf. May be seen standing for a long period of time on one leg, even though it lacks a hind toe. An excellent flyer, aided by ample wing length and sharp, pointed wings. Flocks wheel and turn together in the air. Call is a sharp *kip*, often emitted in a series.

Habitat

Breeds on Arctic and subarctic tundra, west from the Hudson Bay. Migrates in winter to sandy beaches throughout most of Southern Hemisphere, traveling as far as 8,000 miles.

Local Sites

Look for the Sanderling on Florida coastlines during the winter months, feeding wherever surf is strongest.

FIELD NOTES The plumage of the Sanderling is dramatically brighter in the summer than in the winter, when its pale gray blends in with its sandy environment.

Breeding | Adult

LEAST SANDPIPER

Calidris minutilla L 6" (15 cm)

FIELD MARKS

Notably small size

Short, thin bill with slight
downward curve

Streaked, dark neck and breast

Yellowish legs

Behavior

Sandpipers often look like they are chasing waves as
they forage for food, feeding on fish and a wide variety
of invertebrates, such as worms, insects, mollusks, and
small crabs. Watch their yellow legs as they scurry in
across the sand. They are also known to forage in newly
plowed agricultural fields. The Least Sandpiper's call is
characterized by a high *kree*.

Habitat

Common in wetlands and in coastal regions. Breeds in
Arctic regions.

Local Sites

Readily seen throughout Florida in the winter months,
when the bird's plumage shows prominent brown
breast band.

FIELD NOTES The smallest sandpiper in
North America closely resembles the Western Sandpiper, *Calidris mauri* (inset). It has a
slightly larger, tapered bill, arrow-shaped spots on sides, a rufous
wash on back, crown, and ear patch, and black legs and feet.

Nonbreeding | Adults

DUNLIN

Calidris alpina L 8½" (22 cm)

FIELD MARKS
Upperparts grayish brown, breast
gray-brown, belly white

During breeding, back reddish,
underparts offwhite, belly black

Sturdy bill, curved slightly
downward at tip

Behavior
Probes in shallows with a rapid up-down stitching
movement of its sturdy, decurved bill, looking for
insects, larvae, worms, snails, small fish, and small
crustaceans. Short neck makes it appears hunchbacked
during feeding. If breeding grounds are threatened,
male will lift one wing over back in defense. Distinctive
call is a harsh, reedy *kree*.

Habitat
Stays north in the summer, breeding on hummocks or
raised dry areas of the Arctic tundra. Migrates south to
coastal areas and slightly inland for winter months.

Local Sites
For signs of the Dunlin's feeding behavior, keep an
eye out as you visit St. Joseph Peninsula State Park
near Port St. Joe and St. George Island State Park near
Apalachicola, both along the Gulf Coast, during the
winter months.

FIELD NOTES These small but impressive fliers can reach speeds
of over a hundred miles per hour during migration, thanks to
their ample wing length and sharply pointed wings. Traveling in
a large flock, they even perform synchronized maneuvers at
such speeds.

Immature | Juvenile

SHORT-BILLED DOWITCHER

Limnodromus griseus L 11" (28 cm)

FIELD MARKS
Long bill

Distinct pale eyebrow

In winter, brownish gray above,
white below, with gray breast

Juvenile brighter above, buffier
and more spotted below

Behavior
Probes ground for insects with rapid up-down
stitching motion of bill, often submerging head in
water. Roosts in fairly large flocks and interacts with
other species. Short- and Long-billed Dowitchers share
a year-round song of a rapid *di di da doo.* Alarm call is
a mellow *tu tu tu,* repeated in a series. May lock into a
standing position if threatened.

Habitat
Prefers open marshes and mudflats along the coast
during winter months. Nests on subarctic tundra and
grasslands on ground in piled-up bundles of grass
or moss.

Local Sites
Look for the Short-billed Dowitcher in the marshy
wetlands of both coasts, or high in the air around Everglades National Park.

FIELD NOTES The bill of the male Long-billed Dowitcher,
Limnodromus scolopaceus, is no longer than that of the Short-
billed; only the female's grants the species its name. Juveniles
are most easily told apart: The Long-billed juvenile is darker
above, grayer below, and its tertials are plain, lacking the patterned bars, loops, and stripes of the juvenile Short-billed's
tertials. Fall migration begins earlier for the Short-billed as well.

Breeding | Adult

LAUGHING GULL

Larus atricilla L 16½" (42 cm) W 40" (102 cm)

FIELD MARKS
Breeding adult has black hood,
white underparts, slate gray wings
with black outer primaries

In winter, gray wash on nape

Drooping bill

Brown on juvenile head and body

Behavior
Name comes from characteristic call, *ha ha ha ha*,
emitted when feeding or courting. Forages on decayed
fish, crabs, insects, garbage, and anything else it can
get to, sometimes plunging its head underwater. Large
gull flocks can be observed feeding on concentrated
deposits of horseshoe crab eggs in wet sand. Often large
groups congregate around fishing boats, seeking scraps
or discarded offal.

Habitat
Common along coastal regions. Nests of grass and
aquatic plants placed close to each other on sand.

Local Sites
Look for the Laughing Gull year-round on beaches
or slightly inland, wherever a human population
converges. Also common at Merritt Island National
Wildlife Refuge, adjacent to Kennedy Space Center.

FIELD NOTES It takes three years for the Laughing Gull to attain
its full adult plumage. The juvenile has brown on head and body.
By the first winter, although it retains brown wings, its sides and
back turn gray, with a gray wash on the nape. By the second
winter it has lost all brown but still shows a gray wash along the
sides of its breast. Not until the third winter does it develop a
black hood, the sign of a full breeding adult.

Immature | Second-winter

RING-BILLED GULL

Larus delawarensis L 17½" (45 cm) W 48" (122 cm)

FIELD MARKS

Yellow bill with black ring

Pale eye with red ring

Black primaries show white spots

Gray upperparts, white underparts

Yellowish legs and feet

Behavior

Very vocal, Ring-billed Gulls can be heard calling to each other, especially during feeding and nesting. These opportunistic feeders will scavenge the beaches and coastal and inland areas for seeds, grains, grasses, fish, fruit, dead fish, and marine invertebrates.

Habitat

Primarily coastal birds. Will nest in interior regions, but space themselves out along the coastline for the winter. Look for juveniles, which are white with mottled brown up to three years of age.

Local Sites

Abundant and widespread throughout Florida in the winter months, the Ring-billed Gull is usually readily spotted on a pelagic birding trip along the coastline, or even on a visit to the local landfill.

FIELD NOTES Female Ring-billed Gulls have been observed tending nests in pairs or trios when they have successfully mated but have been unable to find a male to pair with.

Breeding | Adult *vegae*

HERRING GULL

Larus argentatus L 25" (64 cm) W 58" (147 cm)

FIELD MARKS

Yellow bill with red mark
near tip

Pale gray mantle in adult

White head streaked with brown
in winter

Pink legs and feet

Behavior

Like other gulls, the Herring Gull forages on land and
in sea for seeds, grains, fruit, shellfish, dead fish, and
marine invertebrates. Will follow a ship at prospect of
refuse thrown overboard. Breaks hard-shelled mollusks
by dropping them onto hard surfaces from high in the
air. Herring Gulls mostly nest in large colonies on the
ground, but they often maintain solitary nests in trees
or on rooftops when necessary. Various calls include
cleew cleew, *kyow*, and *kee-ou kee-ou*. Alarm call is a
quick *kek kek kek*.

Habitat

Primarily a coastal bird, the Herring Gull is numerous
along the Atlantic Coast, but will wander into interior
regions, especially during the winter months and
migration. Look for juveniles, which are overall brown
with dark, two-toned back primaries and tail band in
first year, then gradually change to white by third year.

Local Sites

Winters throughout Florida. May be commonly
sighted at Merritt Island National Wildlife Refuge.

FIELD NOTES The general increase of food sources from landfills,
wastewater treatment plants, and offal from fishing boats has led
to further proliferation of the species, so much so that entire
colonies of terns and other shorebirds have vanished altogether.

Nonbreeding | Adult

ROYAL TERN

Sterna maxima L 20" (51 cm) W 41" (104 cm)

FIELD MARKS

Slim orange-red bill

Black cap, black around eyes in breeding season

White crown most of year

Deeply forked tail

Behavior

Hovers over the water, then plunge-dives after prey including crustaceans and occasionally small toads or frogs. In flight, reveals the pale underside of its primaries. Nests in small depressions in the ground, usually as part of dense colonies. Note that in winter adult and in juvenile, black cap usually does not encompass eye.

Habitat

Prefers coastlines but is known to migrate and winter around inland lakes.

Local Sites

Can be observed year-round along the coastline of the state. During the winter, look for the Royal Tern in interior Florida around Lake Kissimmee and westward toward Sarasota and environs.

FIELD NOTES The Caspian Tern, *Sterna caspia* (inset), is similar to the Royal Tern, but has a much thicker and deeper orange to coral-hued bill, and in flight, the Caspian Tern's primaries show a dark underside.

Breeding | Adult

FORSTER'S TERN

Sterna forsteri L 14½" (37 cm)

FIELD MARKS
Orange-red bill with dark tip

Gray upperparts, white underparts

Orange legs and feet

Long, deeply forked gray tail

Black cap and nape on
breeding adult

Behavior
Forages on insects in flight and on the water's surface.
Hovers over water, then plunge-dives to capture small
fish. In flight, reveals snow-white underparts and
a forked tail with white outer edges. Calls include
a hoarse *kyarr*.

Habitat
Mainly coastal, but also frequents inland marshes. In
nesting areas, look for juveniles with ginger-brown cap,
dark eye patch, and brown spots on wings. Juveniles'
tails are shorter than the adults'.

Local Sites
May be found year-round in the extreme western Panhandle, near Pensacola, and during the winter throughout the state. In winter, look for plumage that is lighter
gray to white and for gray head with elliptical eye
patch.

FIELD NOTES Terns establish monogamous pair bonds, which are
formed through ritualized calling and aerial displays, often initiat-
ed by a male landing near a female and offering her a fish.

Year-round | Adult

LEAST TERN

Sterna antillarum L 9" (23 cm) W 20" (51 cm)

FIELD MARKS
Gray above, black cap and nape, white forehead

Orange-yellow legs and bill, dark tip on bill

Underparts white

Black wedge on outer primaries

Behavior
The smallest of the North American terns, the Least Tern flies rapidly and buoyantly on long, pointed wings. Hovers above, then plunge-dives into water for small fish, crustaceans, and sand eels. Swallows food while flying or delivers it to nest. Calls used for warning or mating include high-pitched *kip* notes and a harsh *chir-ee-eep*. Courtship involves ritualized calling, aerial displays, and offering of fish by male to female.

Habitat
Nests in colonies on beaches and sandbars, also on gravel-filled rooftops near aquatic habitats. Winters from Central America south.

Local Sites
This endangered species can still be found breeding in colonies in the spring and summer months along the causeway to St. George Island State Park. The Least Tern also breeds along the nearby coast of St. Joseph Peninsula State Park near Port St. Joe.

FIELD NOTES A Least Tern sandbar nesting site will relocate with the disappearance and formation of new bars. Ghost Crabs may prey on its nest, and the Least Tern will divebomb such intruders, letting out high-pitched *kip* screeches and attacking with droppings.

Breeding | Adult

BLACK SKIMMER

Rynchops niger L 18" (46 cm) W 44" (112 cm)

FIELD MARKS

Long, red, black-tipped bill

Black back and crown, white face and underparts, red legs

Female distinctly smaller

Juvenile mottled dingy brown

Winter adults show white collar

Behavior

Uses long, pointed wings to glide low over water while dropping its lower mandible to skim the surface for small fish. Once bill touches a small fish or minnow, the maxilla, or upper bill, instantly snaps down to catch prey. Can be found foraging at any time of the day or night. Breeds in colonies, often sharing a site with tern colonies to take advantage of their aggressive defensive tactics. Known to make a yelping bark at nesting colonies or in response to a threat.

Habitat

Prefers sheltered bays, estuaries, coastal marshes, and sometimes inland lakes. Nests in large colonies on barrier islands and salt marshes.

Local Sites

Look for the Black Skimmer breeding alongside the Least Tern on the coast near St. George Island State Park and St. Joseph Peninsula State Park.

FIELD NOTES The Black Skimmer has a distinctive bill: No other known bird has a lower mandible longer than the upper. It also has an adaptive pupil, able to contract to a narrow, vertical slit. This capability is thought to protect the eye from bright sunlight glaring off the water's surface.

Year-round | Adult wildtype

ROCK PIGEON

Columba livia L 12½" (32 cm)

FIELD MARKS
Highly variable in its multicolored
hues, with head and neck usually
darker than back

White rump

Dark band at end of tail

Black bars on inner wing

Behavior
Feeds during the day on grain, seeds, fruit, or refuse
in cities and natural areas, parks and fields. A frequent
visitor to backyard feeding stations as well. As it
forages, the Rock Pigeon moves with a short-stepped,
"pigeon-toed," stodgy gait while its head bobs fore and
aft. Characterized by soft *coo-cuk-cuk-cuk-coooo* call.
Courtship display consists of male turning in circles
while cooing; results in a pairing that could last for life.
Builds nest of stiff twigs, sticks, leaves, and grasses.

Habitat
Widespread throughout U.S. Nests and roosts
primarily on high window ledges, atop bridges, and
in barns.

Local Sites
Look for the Rock Pigeon from urban parks to
country fields, and wherever someone is
willing to spread bread crumbs or
seeds.

FIELD NOTES The White-crowned Pigeon,
Columba leucocephala (inset), is found in the U.S.
only in the Florida Everglades and Keys. Unlike the
variable Rock Pigeon, which ranges from black to
white and most colors in between, the White-crowned is
always an iridescent black with a white crown patch.

Year-round | Adult female

MOURNING DOVE

Zenaida macroura L 12" (31 cm)

FIELD MARKS
Small, pinkish head; black spot
on lower cheek

Trim body; long tail, tapering
to a point

Black spots on upper wing

Brownish-gray upper, pink below

Behavior
Generally ground feeders, Mourning Doves will forage
for grains and other seeds, grasses, and insects. Known
for their mournful call, *oowooo-woo-woo-woo*, given by
males during breeding season. Aggressively territorial,
these doves gather to roost in sheltered groves after
breeding. May breed more than one time each year,
producing as many as six clutches, or even more. Young
are fed regurgitated meal and seeds. Wings produce a
fluttering whistle as the bird takes flight. In flight, white
tips on outer tail feathers are revealed.

Habitat
Widespread and abundant, this dove is found in a variety of habitats, but prefers open areas, often choosing
urban or suburban sites for feeding and nesting,
including front porch eaves.

Local Sites
Widespread throughout Florida, year-round.

FIELD NOTES At 6¼" (17 cm), the Common Ground-Dove, *Columbi-
na passerina* (inset), is barely half the size of the
Mourning Dove. It is found on open ground
and in brushy areas throughout Florida and
is readily identified by its bright chestnut primaries and wing linings,
which are visible in flight.

Year-round | Adult

YELLOW-BILLED CUCKOO

Coccyzus americanus L 12" (31 cm)

FIELD MARKS
Grayish brown above, white
below

Rufous primaries

Yellow lower mandible

Undertail patterned in bold black
and white

Behavior
Unique song sounds hollow and wooden, a rapid
staccato *kuk-kuk-kuk* that usually descends to a
kakakowlp-kowlp ending; heard more often in summer.
This shy species slips quietly through overgrowth,
combing vegetation for caterpillars, frogs, lizards,
cicadas, and other insects. During courtship, male will
climb on female's shoulders to feed her from above.

Habitat
Common in the dense canopies of woods, orchards,
and streamside willow and alder groves throughout
eastern and midwestern U.S. Also inhabits tangles and
vines of marsh and swamp edges. Nests lined with
grasses and moss found on horizontal tree limbs.

Local Sites
Found throughout Florida during spring and summer
breeding period.

FIELD NOTES The closely related and
very rare Mangrove Cuckoo, *Coccyzus
minor* (inset), is found only in Florida,
usually skulking in mangrove thickets along
the Gulf Coast and in the Keys. The black mask and buffy underparts distinguish this species from other cuckoos.

Year-round | Adult male

BARN OWL

Tyto alba L 16" (41 cm)

FIELD MARKS
White heart-shaped face

Dark eyes

Rusty brown upperparts;
cinnamon on back

White to pale cinnamon
underparts

Behavior
A nocturnal forager of mice, small birds, bats, snakes, and insects. Hunts primarily by sound, keeping one ear pointed upwards and one downwards, often in pastures cleared for agriculture. Roosts and nests in dark cavities in city and farm buildings, cliffs, and trees. Chasing, calling, and presenting food by the male are all part of the courtship display. Call is a harsh, raspy, hissing screech.

Habitat
Distributed throughout the world, this owl adapts well to the activities of man and can be found in urban, suburban, farmland, and forest areas throughout its range. Nests are built in a variety of sites such as tree hollows, barn rafters, burrows, and cliff holes.

Local Sites
A year-round resident of Florida. To find an owl, search the ground for regurgitated pellets of fur and bone below a nest or roost. Listen for flocks of small songbirds noisily mobbing a roosting owl.

FIELD NOTES Farmers enjoy the presence of these owls because they are such efficient mousers. They nest at all times of the year, and it is believed that Barn Owls mate for life.

Year-round | Adult

GREAT HORNED OWL

Bubo virginianus L 22" (56 cm)

FIELD MARKS

Notable for overall size; largest owl in Florida

Long, ear tufts (or horns)

Rusty facial disks

Yellow eyes

White chin and throat

Behavior

Chiefly nocturnal, generally becomes active at dusk. Feeds on a wide variety of animals including cats, skunks, porcupines, birds, snakes, and frogs, often attacking prey much larger and heavier than itself. Watches from high perch, then swoops down on prey. Aggressively territorial around nest and young. Call is a series of three to eight loud, deep hoots, the second and third hoots often short and rapid.

Habitat

The most widespread owl in North America, the Great Horned Owl can be found in a wide variety of habitats including forests, cities, farmlands, and open desert. Uses abandoned nests of larger birds, which it finds in trees, caves, on ledges, or on the ground. Normal clutch is two eggs. Tends to nest very early, sometimes even laying eggs in winter.

Local Sites

Common throughout the year in Florida.

FIELD NOTES The Great Horned Owl may be the earliest bird to nest each year, beginning in early January or February, possibly to take advantage of winter-stressed prey and available, ready-made nests of previous birds.

Year-round | Adult red morph

EASTERN SCREECH-OWL

Otus asio L 8½" (22 cm)

FIELD MARKS
Small, with yellow, immobile eyes
and pale bill tip

Underparts marked by vertical
streaks crossed by dark bars

Ear tufts prominent if raised

Round, flattened facial disk

Behavior
Nocturnal owl; uses heightened vision and hearing to
hunt for mice, voles, shrews, and insects. Approached
while roosting during the day, it will elongate body,
erect ear tufts, and close eyes to blend into its back-
ground. Red, gray, and brown morphs exist. Emits a
series of quavering whistles, descending in pitch, or
a long, one-pitch trill.

Habitat
Common in a wide variety of habitats including woodlots, forests, swamps, orchards, parks, and suburban
gardens. Nests in trees about 10 to 30 feet up. Also
known to use man-made nesting boxes.

Local Sites
Look and listen for the red morph of this species in
treetops throughout the state year-round.

FIELD NOTES Like most owls, the Eastern Screech-Owl seeks out
the densest and thickest cover for its daytime roost. To find it,
search the ground for regurgitated pellets of bone and fur, then
look in treetops above. Also listen for flocks of small songbirds
noisily mobbing an owl roost. They are often more likely to find
an owl than you are.

Year-round | Adult

BURROWING OWL

Athene cunicularia L 9½" (24 cm)

FIELD MARKS
Large yellow eyes

White streaks on head, white chin
and throat

Pale underparts with brown bars

Long legs

Short tail

Behavior
Forages primarily at night, dawn, and dusk on insects
and small mammals such as mice. Flight is low and
undulating; can hover like a kestrel. Regularly perches
on the ground or on low posts during the day next to
its burrow. Calls include a soft *co-coooo* and a chattering series of *chack* notes.

Habitat
Open grasslands and prairies, often associated with
prairie dog towns. Has also adapted to man-made
environments such as golf courses and airports.

Local Sites
Year-round resident of Florida from Tallahassee
southward. Look for it in the Keys around the airport
at Marathon.

FIELD NOTES Disturbed in its burrow, the Burrowing Owl often
gives an alarm call that imitates a rattlesnake. It is threatened
over much of its range due to habitat loss, automobile strikes,
and the poisoning of prairie dog towns.

Year-round | Adult

BARRED OWL

Strix varia L 21" (53 cm))

FIELD MARKS
Chunky owl with dark, immobile
eyes in large head

Dark barring on upper breast,
dark streaking below

Long, barred tail

Lacks ear tufts

Behavior
Chiefly nocturnal, the Barred Owl's daytime roost is
always well hidden in deep woods. Its call is more
likely than other owls' to be heard during the day,
consisting of a series of loud hoots: *who-cooks-for-you,
who-cooks-for-you-all.* Also emits a drawn out *hoo-ah,*
sometimes preceded by an ascending, agitated barking.
Has a wide variety of prey, including small mammals,
birds, salamanders, frogs, snakes, lizards, fish, crabs,
and large insects. Catches, holds, and carries prey in its
sharp talons.

Habitat
Prefers dense coniferous or mixed woods around rivers
and swamps; also in upland woods. Range increasing in
Northwest, where it has hybridized with Spotted Owl.
Uses nests or nest boxes abandoned in treetops.

Local Sites
Listen for the Barred Owl's complex and intriguing
calls year-round throughout Florida.

FIELD NOTES Also known as the "hoot owl," the Barred Owl
earns its nickname by routinely using up to ten different calls,
each for a specific purpose. These calls include wails, whines,
squeals, even an eerie laugh. Imitation of its calls can often result
in the owl coming closer and responding.

Year-round | Adult female *sennetti*

COMMON NIGHTHAWK

Chordeiles minor **L** 9½" (24 cm)

FIELD MARKS

Long, pointed wings with pale spotting; tail slightly forked

Bold white bar across primaries, bar on tail in males only; dark, mottled back

Underparts whitish with bold dusky bars, darker in males

Behavior

The Common Nighthawk's streamlined body allows for agile aerial displays when feeding at dusk. Hunts in flight, snaring insects. Capable of dropping lower jaw to create an opening wide enough to scoop in large moths. Roosts on the ground, by scraping a shallow depression in the ground, or on branches, posts, roofs. Call is a nasal *peent*. Throat is white in the male, pale buff in females. Male's white throat may play a role in mating rituals.

Habitat

Seen in woodlands, shrubby areas as well as in towns and even some cities.

Local Sites

May often be seen feeding near bright city lights to which insects are drawn. Common during spring breeding and summer seasons throughout Florida. Migrates as far south as Argentina for the winter.

FIELD NOTES The Common Nighthawk may be observed during daylight hours. It migrates in large flocks. Because of their evening acrobatics, nighthawks are often mistaken for bats, giving rise to a local name of "bullbat."

Year-round | Adult

CHIMNEY SWIFT

Chaetura pelagica L 5¼" (13 cm)

FIELD MARKS
Cigar-shaped body

Short, stubby tail

Dark plumage, sooty gray overall

Long, narrow, curved wings

Blackish gray bill, legs, feet

Behavior
Soars with long wings at great speeds, often in a circle. Catches ants, termites, and spiders while in flight. Groups of Chimney Swifts may circle above a chimney at dusk before dropping in to roost. While perching, emits a high-pitched chattering call; in flight, the call is repeated so quickly that it sounds like a buzz. During aerial courtship, the pursuer raises its wings into a V.

Habitat
Builds cup-shaped nests of small twigs and saliva in chimneys, under eaves of abandoned barns, and in hollow trees. Roosts in chimneys and steeples. Otherwise seen soaring over forested, open, or urban sites. Winters as far south as Peru.

Local Sites
Look for Chimney Swifts soaring above urban and suburban settings throughout the entire state.

FIELD NOTES Before the settlement of North America by Europeans, the Chimney Swift was quite content with nests in hollow trees. It has since adapted so well to artificial nesting sites such as chimneys, air shafts, vertical pipes, barns, and silos, that it has seen a dramatic population increase and is the most common swift in the eastern U.S. and southern Canada.

Year-round | Adult male

RUBY-THROATED HUMMINGBIRD

Archilochus colubris L 3¾" (10 cm)

FIELD MARKS
Metallic green above

Adult male has brilliant red throat, black chin, whitish underparts, dusky green sides

Female has whitish throat, grayish white underparts, buffy wash on sides

Behavior
This species probes backyard hummingbird feeders and flowers for nectar by hovering virtually still in midair. Also feeds on small spiders and insects. When nectar is in short supply, it is known to drink sap from wells made in tree trunks in early spring by sapsuckers. In spring the male Ruby-throateds arrive in breeding territory before the female and engage in jousts to claim prime sites. Once mated, females build nests on small tree limbs and raise young by themselves.

Habitat
Found in gardens and woodland edges throughout most of eastern United States.

Local Sites
Known to breed south of Lake Okeechobee. Listen for the humming of its wings in gardens, flowering hedges, and blooming fields.

FIELD NOTES Hummingbirds and the flowers they pollinate have both adapted to meet each other's needs. Typical flowers favored by the hummingbird are narrow and tubular, the nectar accessible only to a long bill or tongue. Hummingbirds are attracted to bright red, orange, and pink, and flowers' subtle color patterns may signal nectar availability to the birds.

Year-round | Adult female

BELTED KINGFISHER

Ceryle alcyon L 13" (33 cm)

FIELD MARKS

Blue-gray head with large, shaggy crest, blue-gray upperparts and breast band

Long, heavy black bill

White collar and underparts

Chestnut sides and belly band in female

Behavior
Generally solitary and vocal, dives for fish from a water-side perch or after hovering above in order to line up on its target. Will also feed on insects, amphibians, and small reptiles. Call is a loud, dry rattle, often given when alarmed, to announce territory, or while in flight. The Kingfisher is one of few birds in North America in which the female is more colorful than the male, which lacks the female's chestnut band across the belly, sides, and flanks.

Habitat
Common and conspicuous along rivers, ponds, lakes, coasts, and estuaries. Prefers areas that are partially wooded.

Local Sites
Resides year-round in the northern half of Florida and winters from Tampa southward. These fish-eaters are at the Paynes Prairie State Preserve or along Lake George.

FIELD NOTES Kingfisher pairs are monogamous and nest in burrows that they dig three or more feet into vertical, earthen banks near suitable watery habitats. Both sexes build the nest and share parenting duties for their clutches of three to eight. Mated pairs renew their relationship with each breeding season, using courtship rituals such as dramatic display flights, the feeding of the female by the male, and vocalizations.

Year-round | Adult

RED-BELLIED WOODPECKER

Melanerpes carolinus L 9¼" (24 cm)

FIELD MARKS

Black and white barred back

White uppertail coverts

Central tail feathers barred

Red nape; red crown only
on males

Small reddish tinge on belly

Behavior

Climbs tree trunks by bracing itself with stiff tail,
taking strain off short legs. Uses chisel-shaped bill
to drill cavities in and through tree bark and extract
grubs, worms, fruits, and seeds. Also known to feed on
sap from wells made by sapsuckers, and on sunflower
seeds and peanut butter in feeders. Call is a whirring
churr or *chiv-chiv* that rises and falls, reminiscent of
the whirring of wings.

Habitat

Common in open woodlands, forest edges, suburbs,
and parks. Breeding range extends northward. Nests
and roosts at night in tree cavities.

Local Sites

Try for a view of the Red-bellied Woodpecker returning
to its roost in the tall pines of Apalachicola National
Forest, southwest of Tallahassee.

FIELD NOTES Like other woodpeckers, during breeding the
Red-bellied uses both calls and nonvocal drumming, made by
pecking hard wood repeatedly with its bill. But unlike the calls of
songbirds, this courtship display is common among both the
male and female. The bone and muscle structures of these
woodpeckers have adapted to become shock absorbers,
necessary for their habit of pecking at tree trunks.

Year-round | Adult "Yellow-shafted"

NORTHERN FLICKER

Colaptes auratus L 12½" (32 cm)

FIELD MARKS
Brown, barred back, cream under-parts with black spotting and black crescent bib

Gray crown, tan face with red crescent on nape and, on male, black moustachial stripe

White rump, yellowish underwing

Behavior
Feeds mostly on the ground, primarily on ants, but is a cavity-nesting bird that will drill into aboveground wooden surfaces including utility poles and houses. Call is a long, loud series of *wick-er, wick-er* on the breeding ground, or a single, loud *klee-yer* year-round.

Habitat
Prefers open woodlands and suburban areas with sizeable living and dead trees. As insectivores, Northern Flickers are at least partially migratory, moving south-ward in the winter in pursuit of food.

Local Sites
Commonly found throughout Florida's woodland areas year-round. Look for them in old-growth bottomland forests, a preferred habitat.

FIELD NOTES Two distinct groups make up the Northern Flicker species. The "Red-shafted Flicker" is more often seen in the western U.S. The "Yellow-shafted Flicker," described above, is less often seen in the West, rarely in fall and winter, but is more commonly seen in the eastern and northern United States.

Year-round | Adult

DOWNY WOODPECKER

Picoides pubescens L 6¾" (17 cm)

FIELD MARKS
White belly, back, outer tailfeathers

Black, stubby bill

Black marlar stripe, black cap and ear patch; red occipital patch on male only

Black wings with white spots

Behavior
Smallest woodpecker in North America; forages mainly on insects, larvae, and insect eggs. Will also eat seeds and readily visits backyard feeders for sunflower seeds and suet. Known to consume poison ivy berries. Call is a high-pitched but soft *pik*. Note the dull spots or bars on the white outer tailfeathers.

Habitat
Common in suburbs, parks, and orchards as well as in forests and woodlands.

Local Sites
A year-round resident of Florida, these unwary insectivores are usually easily spotted throughout their range.

FIELD NOTES The larger Hairy Woodpecker, *Picoides villosus* (inset), is similarly marked but has a bill as long as its head and unmarked white outer tail feathers. Young males of this species show spots of white on the forehead and a crown streaked with red or orange.

Year-round | Adult female

Picoides borealis L 8½" (22 cm)

WOODPECKERS

FIELD MARKS
Black-and-white barred back

Black forehead, cap, and nape

White cheek patches

Red tufts, usually invisible, on male's head

Whitish underparts

Behavior
Forages and drills for insects in pine trunks, sometimes moving up tree in spiral fashion. Also forages on berries and nuts and on earworms in corn in summer. A cooperative breeder, the Red-cockaded is often seen in a clan of three to seven, consisting of a mated pair, nestlings, and unmated adult helpers. Calls consist of a buzzy, raspy *sripp* and a high-pitched *tsick*.

Habitat
Inhabits open, mature pine or pine-oak woodlands of the southeast where unlogged stands of 80-90 year-old trees remain. Requires a living pine tree for nesting, as pine pitch oozing from holes may repel predators.

Local Sites
This endangered species can still be found nesting in summer at Apalachicola National Forest, a center of the now-dwindling population.

FIELD NOTES In summer, male begins to bore a nest hole into living pines afflicted with heartwood disease, then drills small holes around the nest opening. These constructions take more than a year to complete, but can be reused for forty to fifty years by a variety of other animals including other birds, flying squirrels, snakes, mice, and insects. These cavities also serve as distinctive signposts for humans.

Year-round | Adult male

PILEATED WOODPECKER

Dryocopus pileatus L 16½" (42 cm)

FIELD MARKS

Almost entirely black on back
and wings when perched

White chin and dark bill

Red cap full in male, less
extensive in female

Juvenile plumage duller

Behavior

Excavates long rectangular or oval holes, then feeds on
insects that sap attracts. Also digs into ground, stumps,
and fallen logs, feeding extensively on carpenter ants,
beetles, acorns, nuts, seeds, and fruits. Call is a loud
wuck note or series of notes, but better known by its
loud territorial drumming, which sounds like a tree
being hit by a wooden mallet. A single sequence of
drumming sounds diminishes in amplitude and
increases in frequency as it goes along. The Pileated
Woodpecker's loud, resonant drumming can be heard
from distances of a mile or more away.

Habitat

Prefers dense, mature forests; also found in woodlots
and parklands. Nests in a cavity excavated from a dead
or live tree, sometimes even in a utility pole.

Local Sites

Heard, and occasionally seen, among the large bald
cypresses of Fakahatchee Strand State Preserve on the
Gulf Coast.

FIELD NOTES A close relative, the Ivory-billed Woodpecker,
Campephilus principalis, distinguished by its black chin and ivory
bill, is presumed to be extinct. Recent unverified reports have led
to search efforts in Louisiana and Arkansas, yet results have
been inconclusive.

Year-round | Adult

EASTERN KINGBIRD

Tyrannus tyrannus L 8½" (22 cm)

FIELD MARKS
Black head, slate gray back

White terminal band on tail

Underparts white, pale gray wash across breast

Orange-red crown patch visible only when displaying

Behavior
Waits on perch until it sees an insect, then catches prey in midair and returns to perch to eat. Feeds during winter almost exclusively on flying insects, but may also hover and pick fruits or berries off ground. Raspy call when feeding or defending, sounds like *zeer;* also uses a harsh *dzeet* note alone or in a series. Males court through erratic hovering, swooping, and circling, revealing otherwise hidden crown patch.

Habitat
Common and conspicuous in woodland clearings with small forest stands, farms, and orchards. Builds cup-shaped nest of weeds, moss, and feathers near the end of a horizontal tree branch, sometimes on a post or stump. Winters in South America, where it subsists mostly on berries.

Local Sites
The Eastern Kingbird can be observed perched on wire fences, on treetops, or near water in the winter months throughout the peninsula and Panhandle.

FIELD NOTES Living up to its Latin name, which means "tyrant of tyrants,"the Eastern Kingbird will actively defend its nest, sometimes pecking at and even pulling feathers from the backs of hawks, crows, and vultures.

Year-round | Adult *maynardi*

Vireo griseus L 5" (13 cm)

FIELD MARKS

Grayish olive above

White below, pale yellow sides and flanks

Two whitish wing bars

Yellow spectacles and distinctive white iris visible at close range

Behavior

Thick, blunt, mildly hooked bill for catching flies and gleaning fruits and berries. May be seen in mixed foraging flocks during migration. The White-eyed Vireo is characterized by its loud, grating, jumbled, five- to seven-note call, usually beginning and ending with a sharp *chick*. The notes run together, the middle portion seeming to mimic other birds' songs. Though regional and individual variations abound, the standard, accepted sequence is *quick-with-the-beer-check*! The White-eyed is also known to sing into the heat of the summer, when other birds stay quiet. During breeding season, female wanders territories of males until a suitable mate is found.

Habitat

Prefers to conceal itself close to the ground in dense thickets, brushy tangles, and forest overgrowth.

Local Sites

White-eyed Vireos may be found at woods' edges in the Apalachicola National Forest, southwest of Tallahassee.

FIELD NOTES The subspecies *Vireo griseus maynardi* is found only in the Florida Keys. It is distinguished from other subspecies by grayer upperparts, less yellow underparts, and a larger bill.

Breeding | Adult

RED-EYED VIREO

Vireo olivaceus L 6" (15 cm)

FIELD MARKS
Blue-gray crown

White eyebrow bordered above
and below in black

Olive back, darker wings and tail

White underparts

Ruby red eye, visible at close range

Behavior
Forages through foliage for fruits, berries, and
especially caterpillars. Sometimes hovers to snatch food
from high branch. Song is a variable series of deliberate, short phrases, sung nearly without end from dawn
through dusk and often all night as well, while brooding, foraging, roosting, even while swallowing. Male
known to chase female during courtship, sometimes
even pinning her to the ground.

Habitat
Common in the forest canopies of eastern deciduous
woodlands. Builds nests on horizontal tree limbs,
constructing them of grass and forest debris.

Local Sites
Look, but especially listen, for the Red-eyed Vireo
north of Lake Okeechobee during winter months.

FIELD NOTES The Black-whiskered
Vireo, *Vireo altiloquus* (inset), found
in mangrove swamps of the Florida
Keys, is difficult to distinguish from the Red-eyed
by looks alone. It has even the same ruby red iris.
One way is by its songs, deliberate one- to four-note phrases,
less varied and stronger than those of the Red-eyed.

Year-round | Adult

BLUE JAY

Cyanocitta cristata L 11" (28 cm)

FIELD MARKS
Dull blue crest and back

Black barring and white patches
on blue wings and tail

Black necklace on whitish
underparts

Bristles cover nostrils

Behavior
Noisy, bold Blue Jays are noted for their loud, piercing
call of *jay jay jay* when alarmed, their musical *weedle-
eedle*, and their imitations of several hawk species. A
two-note vocalization and a bobbing display may be
observed during courting. Often seen in small family
groups, foraging for insects, nuts, and berries. Blue Jays
are also known to organize into large feeding flocks to
raid nests for eggs and nestlings of other species.

Habitat
Once primarily a deciduous forest dweller, the Blue
Jay has adapted to fragmented woodlands, parks,
suburban backyards, even cities. Builds nests of twigs,
bark, moss, and discarded paper or string in oak and
beech trees 5- to 20- feet up.

Local Sites
Blue Jays can be spotted year-round throughout most
of Florida. If not found in your backyard, try more
wooded areas like Avon Park Air Force Range.

FIELD NOTES A resourceful feeder, Blue Jays are also known to
store acorns in the ground for winter. This practice becomes a
major factor in the establishment and distribution of oak forests,
further helping the jays' own cause.

Year-round | Adult

FLORIDA SCRUB-JAY

Aphelocoma coerulescens L 11" (28 cm)

FIELD MARKS
Whitish forehead and eyebrow

Short, broad bill

Pale back, distinct collar

Indistinct streaking below

Long tail

Behavior
Known to stash such bright items as forks, glassware, and jewelry when possible. Stores acorns and nuts as well in the ground, covering them with leaves and stones. Hops on ground to forage, eating wide variety of mice, eggs, insects, scorpions, and turtles. In a cooperative breeding system, juveniles from the previous year or other nonbreeding adults may stay around to help parents protect and feed young. Varied calls include raspy, hoarse notes.

Habitat
Optimum habitat is transitional, produced by fire, consisting of scrub, mainly oak, about ten feet high with small openings. Found only in central Florida.

Local Sites
Known to nest at Merritt Island National Wildlife Refuge, where individuals may take food right from your hand.

FIELD NOTES The threatened Florida Scrub-Jay is a fragile and finicky species, insisting on a specialized habitat that has become small and fragmented due to continued development. Rarely wandering more than a mile from its hatch site, it is unwilling to explore far enough from home to find other areas with the right kind of scrub. This species declined some 90 percent during the 20th century.

Year-round | Adult

AMERICAN CROW

Corvus brachyrhynchos L 17½" (45 cm)

FIELD MARKS

Long, heavy, black bill, smaller than raven's

Black, iridescent plumage

Fan-shaped tail in flight, distinguishable from raven's

Familiar *caw* call

Behavior

Omnivorous. Often forages, roosts, and travels in flocks. Individuals take turns at sentry duty and feed on insects, garbage, grain, mice, eggs, and baby birds. Regularly seen noisily mobbing large predators like eagles, hawks, and Great Horned Owls. Since bills are not effective in tearing through hides, crows wait for another predator—or an automobile—to open a carcass before they dine on it. Recognizable call of *caw caw*. Studies have shown the crow's ability to count, solve puzzles, and retain information.

Habitat

Among the most widely distributed and familiar birds in North America.

Local Sites

Common throughout the state but especially viewable in the vicinity of landfill and agricultural operations.

FIELD NOTES The related Fish Crow, *Corvus ossifragus* (inset), is smaller than American Crow with a longer tail, smaller head and bill, stiff wing beats, and a two-syllable *ca-hah* call.

Breeding | Adult

TREE SWALLOW

Tachycineta bicolor L 5¾" (15 cm)

FIELD MARKS
Dark, glossy greenish blue above, white below

Juveniles gray-brown above

White cheek patch; does not extend above eye

Slightly notched tail

Behavior
Often seen in huge flocks, especially during migration and in winter. Forages on insects in flight and changes to a diet of berries or plant buds during colder months, when insects are less abundant. Plumage changes to more of a greenish hue in the fall.

Habitat
Common in wooded habitats near water or where dead trees provide nest holes. Also favors nesting in man-made birdhouses.

Local Sites
A migratory bird, the Tree Swallow is most often seen in Florida during the fall and over the winter. Watch for these skillful insect-catchers at Merritt Island National Wildlife Refuge.

FIELD NOTES Among the world's swallows, the Tree Swallow more regularly feeds on plant material and has a particular fondness for waxy bayberries, for which it has developed a special digesting ability. These adaptations allow it to migrate north sooner and linger later in the fall.

Year-round | Adult male

PURPLE MARTIN

Progne subis L 8" (20 cm)

FIELD MARKS
Dark, glossy purplish blue

Female, juvenile gray below

Forked tail

Fluid flight, short glides
alternating with rapid flapping

Behavior
Forages almost exclusively in flight, darting for wasps,
bees, dragonflies, winged ants, and other large insects.
Long, sharply pointed wings and a substantial tail
allow it graceful maneuverability in the air, but feet
and legs are small so it walks with a weak, shuffling
gait. Capable of drinking, even bathing, in flight by
skimming just over water's surface and dipping bill,
or breast, into water.

Habitat
Common in summer where suitable nest sites are
available, such as woodpecker holes in trees and cacti,
ridges in cliffs or large rocks, and man-made multi-
dwelling Martin houses.

Local Sites
Look for flocks in the summer perched in long rows on
branches and wires throughout the state.

FIELD NOTES Eastern Purple Martins are highly dependent on
man-made nesting houses, which can be filled with hundreds of
pairs of breeding adults. The tradition of making Martin houses
from hollowed gourds originated with Native Americans, who
found that this sociable bird helped reduce insects around
villages and crops. The practice was adopted by colonists as
well. Martins have accordingly prospered for many generations.

Year-round | Adult male

BARN SWALLOW

Hirundo rustica L 6¾" (17 cm)

FIELD MARKS
Long, deeply forked tail
Reddish brown throat
Dark blue-black breast band
Iridescent blue upperparts
Cinnamon to buff underparts

Behavior
An exuberant flyer, often seen in small flocks. Catches flying insects in mid-air as it skims low over the surface of a field or pond. Will follow tractors and lawn mowers to feed on the flushed insects.

Habitat
Open farms and fields, especially near water. Has adapted to the presence of people to the extent that it now nests almost exclusively in structures such as barns, bridges, culverts, and garages, in pairs or small colonies. Bowl-shaped nests are made of mud and grass, lined with feathers.

Local Sites
Can be seen during migration throughout the state. Breeds in all but the extreme southeast portion of the peninsula. Departs in fall on lengthy flights to wintering grounds in Central and South America.

FIELD NOTES The juvenile Barn Swallow has pale underparts and a noticeably shorter tail, still with characteristic fork. The world's most widely distributed swallow, it is common and abundant throughout Europe and Asia and winters in southern Africa and South America.

Year-round | Adult

CAROLINA CHICKADEE

Poecile carolinensis L 4¾" (12 cm)

FIELD MARKS
Black cap and bib

Lower edge of bib sharply defined

White cheeks, gray upperparts

Whitish underparts with buff-gray
wash on flanks and lower belly

Behavior
Seldom descending to ground, energetically forages
among leaves and twigs for moths, caterpillars, and
insects. Often hangs upside down to glean underside
of foliage. Visits backyard feeders for seeds and suet.
Best distinguished from Black-capped Chickadee by
call. A higher, faster version of *chick-a-dee-dee-dee*,
song is a four-note whistle: *fee-bee fee-bay*.

Habitat
Clearings and edges of mixed woodlands, open oak
forests, wooded city parks, and urban thickets. Known
to hybridize with Black-capped Chickadee in areas
where their habitats overlap. Nests in old woodpecker
holes, man-made nesting boxes, and natural crevices.

Local Sites
Permanent resident of the pine woods and oak forests
north of Lake Okeechobee. Absent in southern Florida
and the Keys.

FIELD NOTES When alarmed on the nest, the Carolina Chickadee
will hiss and strike in snakelike fashion. After the breeding
season it joins in mixed foraging flocks with nuthatches,
warblers, Downy Woodpeckers, and other small birds.

Year-round | Adult

TUFTED TITMOUSE

Baeolophus bicolor L 6¼" (16 cm)

FIELD MARKS
Gray crest

Distinct blackish forehead

Gray upperparts

Russet wash on sides

Whitish underparts

Behavior
Very active forager in trees, seeking insects, sometimes hanging upside down while feeding. May also be seen holding a nut in its feet and pounding it with its bill. A common visitor to backyard feeders, especially fond of sunflower seeds and suet. Stores surplus feed underground. Male feeds female in courtship. Primary song is a loud, whistled *peter peter peter*, but it also employs up to ten groups of calls.

Habitat
Open forests, woodlands, groves, and orchards, as well as urban and suburban parks with large trees and shrubs. Nests in natural cavities, woodpecker holes, man-made boxes, sometimes in fenceposts near open pastures surrounded by wooded areas.

Local Sites
Resident throughout the peninsula and Panhandle but absent in southeastern Florida and the Keys.

FIELD NOTES Unintimidated by proximity to humans, the Tufted Titmouse will fly toward people and make a squeaking sound or *pish* to attract more birds. It is known to swoop down and pluck hair directly from a human's scalp for use in its nest. It may also learn to eat from a human hand.

Year-round | Adult

BROWN-HEADED NUTHATCH

Sitta pusilla L 4½" (11 cm)

FIELD MARKS
Brown cap

Blue-gray upperparts

Dull buff underparts

Pale nape spot visible at close range

Dark, narrow eyeline borders cap

Behavior
Small and usually noisy nuthatch that feeds in pairs or small flocks. Forages in pine tree bark for insects, using one piece of bark to dislodge another. Also picks seeds from pinecones, especially in winter. Call is a repeated double note like the squeak of a rubber duck. Feeding flocks also give twittering *bit bit bit* calls. Known to form flocks with chickadees and warblers.

Habitat
Fairly widespread. Frequently to be found in open pine woods.

Local Sites
Sparse in southeastern Florida south of Lake Okeechobee. Look for this nuthatch high in trees, well out on their branches, at Ocala National Forest and at Morningside Nature Center, east of the University of Florida in Gainesville. Does not frequent the Keys.

FIELD NOTES The White-breasted Nuthatch, *Sitta carolinensis* (inset), was once widespread throughout Florida, but for reasons not fully understood its population has decreased over the past decades and is now found only in northern Florida, especially in Tall Timbers Research Station and Phipps/Overstreet Park in Tallahassee.

Year-round | Adult *aedon*

HOUSE WREN

Troglodytes aedon L 4¾" (12 cm)

FIELD MARKS
Faint eyebrow

Thin, slightly decurved bill

Grayish brown upperparts

Pale gray underparts

Fine black barring on wings
and tail

Behavior
Noisy, conspicuous, and relatively tame, with a tail
often cocked upward. Boldly gleans insects, spiders,
and snails from vegetation. While most species of wren
forage low to the ground, the House Wren will seek
food at a variety of levels, including high in the trees.
Sings exuberantly in a cascade of bubbling whistled
notes. Call is a rough *cheh cheh*, often running together
into a chatter.

Habitat
Highly tolerant of human presence, hence common in
shrubbery around farms, parks, and urban gardens.

Local Sites
A migratory bird that spends the spring and summer
months in the mid-Atlantic and northern parts of the
United States and is resident throughout Florida in
the winter months.

FIELD NOTES The House Wren is very competitive when searching
for nest sites. It often invades the nests of other songbirds,
punctures their eggs, and kills their young in order to take over
the nest. Once a territory is established, the male will begin building his own nests in every available opening, from natural cavities
to birdhouses to boots, cans, buckets, mailboxes, and coat
pockets. One nest is selected to be completed by the female.

Year-round | Adult

CAROLINA WREN

Thryothorus ludovicianus L 5½" (14 cm)

FIELD MARKS
Deep rusty brown above

Warm buff below

Prominent white eye stripe

White throat

Long, slightly decurved bill

Behavior
Pokes into every nook and cranny on the ground with its decurved bill, looking for insects, spiders, snails, millipedes, fruits, berries, and seeds. May also eat small lizards and tree frogs. From an exposed perch at any time of day or year, male sings melodious *teakettle tea-kettle teakettle* or *cheery cheery cheery*, to which female often responds with a growl of *t-shihrrr*. A pair stays together in its territory throughout the year.

Habitat
Common in concealing underbrush of moist woodlands and swamps and around human habitation on farms and in wooded suburbs. Nests in any open cavity of suitable size, including old woodpecker holes in trees or stumps, bird boxes, barn rafters, mailboxes, flower pots, even boots left outside.

Local Sites
The Carolina Wren is a loud and conspicuous year-round resident throughout Florida.

FIELD NOTES The Carolina Wren is very picky about temperature. It remains year-round throughout its range except after mild winters, when its range expands northward, or after harsh winters, when its range retracts southward.

Year-round | Adult

MARSH WREN

Cistothorus palustris L 5" (13 cm)

FIELD MARKS
Black cap, bold white eye stripe

Warm brown upperparts with black and white streaking

Rufous sides, flanks and undertail coverts

Long, slender bill

Behavior
Secretively forages among marsh reeds and grasses for insects, larvae, snails, and, occasionally, other birds' eggs. May be seen alone, with a mate, or in a small colony, depending on the girth and quality of the habitat. Males may sing from exposed perch before heading back under cover of vegetation. Call combines liquid notes with slightly harsh tones and can result in up to 219 different songs. When alarmed by intruder, call is a sharp *tsuk,* often doubled.

Habitat
Common to, but stays hidden in, reedy marshes and cattail swamps.

Local Sites
Like most wrens, the Marsh Wren is often heard before it is seen. Look for it perching atop tall marsh reeds in swampy areas, year-round along both the east and Gulf coasts of Florida and during winter in the interior of the state.

FIELD NOTES The male constructs several spherical nests with side entrances. From them, the female will choose one to finish for incubation. Frequently a male roosts in one of the dummy nests while tending to multiple mates.

Breeding | Adult male

BLUE-GRAY GNATCATCHER

Polioptila caerulea L 4½" (11 cm)

FIELD MARKS

Male is blue-gray above, female is grayer

Black line on sides of crown in breeding plumage only

Long, black tail with white outer feathers

Behavior

Scours deciduous tree limbs and leaves for small insects or spiders, otherwise sometimes captures prey in flight. May hover briefly. Distinguished by its high-pitched buzz while feeding or breeding. Also emits a querulous *pwee*. Known for scratchy imitations of other birds' songs, a surprise to birders expecting this only from the Mimidae family.

Habitat

Favors woodlands, thickets, and lowland chaparral. Male and female together make cuplike nest of plant fibers, spider webs, moss, and lichen. A disturbance at the nest site early on will cause the couple to depart and rebuild elsewhere.

Local Sites

Florida is one of the few places in the U.S. where the Blue-gray Gnatcatcher can be seen in the winter. Look for them in summer as well, near bodies of water north of Lake Okeechobee.

FIELD NOTES Like some other species, gnatcatchers are born altricial: that is, they are born naked and unable to see. The young are fed in the nest for about two weeks, then outside for another three weeks.

Year-round | Adult male

EASTERN BLUEBIRD

Sialia sialis L 7" (18 cm)

FIELD MARKS

Chestnut throat, breast, sides
and side of neck

White belly and undertail coverts

Male is uniformly deep blue
above

Female is grayer blue above

Behavior

Tends to still-hunt from an elevated perch in the open,
dropping to the ground to seize crickets, grasshoppers,
and spiders. With incredibly acute eyes, the Eastern
Bluebird has been observed pouncing on prey spotted
from 130 feet away. Call note is a musical, rising
chur-lee, extended in song to *chur chur-lee chur-lee*.
Often forms large flocks and roosts communally in
tree cavities or nest boxes by night. During courtship,
male will make floating butterfly and wing-waving
displays beside a chosen nesting site.

Habitat

Found in open woodlands, meadows, farmlands, and
orchards. Nests with grass, stems, twigs, and needles in
holes in trees and posts, and in nest boxes.

Local Sites

The Eastern Bluebird flies only as far south as it needs
to find food, therefore found year-round throughout
Florida except in the southern tip and in the Keys.

FIELD NOTES Serious decline in recent decades is due largely to
competition with the European Starling and the House Sparrow
for nesting sites. The provision of specially designed nesting
boxes by a concerned birding community has resulted in a
promising comeback.

Year-round | Adult female

AMERICAN ROBIN

Turdus migratorius L 10" (25 cm)

FIELD MARKS

Gray-brown above with darker head and tail

Yellow bill

White under chin

Brick red underparts

White lower belly

Behavior

Best known and largest of the thrushes. Often seen on suburban lawns, hopping about and cocking its head to one side in search of earthworms. The American Robin will also glean foliage for butterflies, damselflies, and other insects, and may take such prey in flight. Robins also consume fruit, usually in the fall and winter. This broad plant and animal diet makes them one of the most successful and wide-ranging thrushes.

Habitat

Widespread, seen in grassy lawns. Nests in shrubs, woodlands, swamps, and parks.

Local Sites

A permanent resident of the Panhandle of Florida. spreads further south into the rest of the state during the winter.

FIELD NOTES The juvenile robin has a paler breast, like the female of the species, but its underparts are tinged with cinnamon and heavily spotted with brown and its wings are tipped with white.

Year-round | Adult

GRAY CATBIRD

Dumetella carolinensis L 8½" (22 cm)

FIELD MARKS
Dark gray overall

Black cap

Long, black tail, often cocked

Undertail coverts chestnut

Short, dark bill

Behavior
Got its name from copying the harsh, downslurred *mew* of a cat interspersed within a variable mixture of melodious, nasal, and squeaky, sometimes abrasive but never repeated, notes. Also known to jump abruptly from one phrase to another. Stays low in thick brush, foraging by walking on strong legs, gleaning insects, spiders, berries, and fruit from branches, foliage, and the ground.

Habitat
Tends to stay hidden in low, dense thickets of undergrowth in woodlands and residential areas. Female builds nest in low shrubs or in small trees with dense growth that offers some protection.

Local Sites
Look for the Gray Catbird associated within a loose flock of other species only in the winter months throughout all of Florida. No other bird in Florida is dark gray above and below with a long tail.

FIELD NOTES In addition to the *mew* sounds mimicked from cats, the Gray Catbird is capable of reproducing the sounds of other birds, of amphibians, even of machinery, and incorporating them into its song.

Year-round | Adult

NORTHERN MOCKINGBIRD

Mimus polyglottos L 10" (25 cm)

FIELD MARKS
Gray plumage, dark wings and tail

White wing patches and outer
tail feathers flash conspicuously
during flight

Repeats same phrase several
times while singing

Behavior
This popular, widespread mimic is known for its
variety of song, learning as many as 200. Males have a
spring and fall song repertoire. Highly pugnacious, it
will protect its territory against not only other birds
but also dogs, cats, and even humans. Has a varied
diet that includes grasshoppers, spiders, snails, and
earthworms.

Habitat
Resides in a variety of habitats, including in towns and
near human habitations. Feeds close to the ground, in
thickets or heavy vegetation.

Local Sites
Wide-ranging, the Northern Mockingbird is a year-
round resident throughout Florida. Difficult to locate,
but listen for their characteristic repeating
of song phrases three times before
beginning a new one.

FIELD NOTES The Loggerhead Shrike,
Lanius ludovicianus (inset), L 9" (23 cm),
though not related, looks strikingly
like the Northern Mockingbird, but
note the black mask and hooked bill of
this falconlike songbird. In flight, wings and tail are
darker and white wing patches are smaller than those of the
Northern Mockingbird.

Year-round | Adult

BROWN THRASHER

Toxostoma rufum L 11½" (29 cm)

FIELD MARKS
Reddish-brown above

Heavily streaked below

Yellow eyes

Long, reddish-brown tail

Immature's eyes may be gray
or brown

Behavior
Forages on or near ground for fruit and grain; finds
insects and small amphibians by digging with decurved
bill. Song is a long series of varied melodious phrases,
each phrase given two or three times. Calls include a
smack and a *churr*. Courtship involves very little fan-
fare; the whole process consists of one or both birds
picking up some leaves or twigs and dropping it in
front of the other.

Habitat
Common in hedgerows, brush, and woodland edges.
Often close to human habitation, having adapted to
living in the vegetation of the ornamental shrubs of
suburban gardens. Nests in bushes, on ground, or in
low trees.

Local Sites
The Brown Thrasher is fairly common and widespread
year-round in places of sizeable vegetation throughout
the state of Florida.

FIELD NOTES A highly creative bird, the Brown Thrasher has the
ability to mimic other birds, but more often sings its own song;
it's got enough of them. It has been reproted that the Brown
Thrasher has the largest song repertoire of all North American
birds; more than 1,100 types have been recorded.

Nonbreeding | Adult

EUROPEAN STARLING

Sturnus vulgaris L 8½" (22 cm)

FIELD MARKS

Speckled plumage, iridescent black during breeding

Yellow bill with pink base in female, blue in male

In fall, brownish bill and feathers tipped in white and buff

Behavior

A highly social and aggressive bird, the European Starling will gorge on a tremendous variety of food, ranging from invertebrates—snails, worms, spiders—to fruits, berries, grains, seeds, and even garbage. Will imitate songs of other species and has call notes that include squeaks, warbles, chirps, and twittering.

Habitat

Adaptable starlings thrive in a variety of habitats, from urban centers to agricultural regions. They nest in cavities ranging from crevices in urban settings to woodpecker holes and nest boxes.

Local Sites

Widespread, the European Starling is a year-round resident of Florida.

FIELD NOTES A Eurasian species introduced to America in the 1890s that has since spread throughout the U. S. and Canada. Abundant, bold, and aggressive, European Starlings often compete for and take over nest sites of other birds, including Eastern Bluebirds, Wood Ducks, Red-bellied Woodpeckers, Great Crested Flycatchers, and Purple Martins.

Year-round | Adult male

NORTHERN PARULA

Parula americana L 4½" (11 cm)

FIELD MARKS

Gray-blue above with yellowish-green upper back

Two bold white wing bars

Throat and breast bright yellow

Adult male shows reddish and black breast bands

Behavior

A very active forager, the Northern Parula can be observed upside down on tree trunks seeking out larvae; hovering in search of caterpillars or spiders, for which its beak is well adapted; or in aerial pursuit of flying insects. Song can be heard from the treetops during nesting or migration, consisting of a rising, buzz-like trill, which ends with an abrupt *zip* in the eastern birds.

Habitat

Common in coniferous or mixed woods, especially near water. Nests in trees covered with either Spanish moss or the lichen *Usnea*.

Local Sites

The Northern Parula winters in Florida from Lake Okeechobee south, including the Keys, resides from about Okeechobee to Orlando, and breeds throughout the northern peninsula and the panhandle. Look for nests hanging from trees on moss or vines at Fort Pickens on Santa Rosa Island.

FIELD NOTES The Tropical Parula, *Parula pitiayumi*, is a similar size and has a song nearly identical to the Northern Parula. Where their ranges overlap in southern Texas and points further south, the Tropical is distinguished by a lack of a white eye ring, and in the males by a lack of reddish and black breast bands.

Breeding | Adult male "Myrtle"

YELLOW-RUMPED WARBLER

Dendroica coronata L 5½" (14 cm)

FIELD MARKS
Bright yellow rump

Yellow patch on sides

Yellow crown patch

White wing bars and tail patches

Females and fall males duller than
breeding males

Behavior
Easy to locate and observe darting about branches
from tree to tree, foraging for insects and spiders in
the spring and summer, for myrtle berries and seeds
in winter. Also drinks tree sap and juice from fallen
oranges. Courtship involves intensive singing. Nest-
building and incubation carried out mainly by the
female. Songs of the eastern subspecies include a slow
warble and a musical trill.

Habitat
Abundant in coniferous or mixed woodlands. Nests
discreetly and solitarily on fork or branch of tree.

Local Sites
Look for the white, black, and yellow underparts of the
Yellow-rumped in winter throughout Florida. Pay particular attention in early pring and fall, when immense
flocks may be seen migrating during the day.

FIELD NOTES The eastern subspecies of the Yellow-rumped
Warbler is often referred to as "Myrtle Warbler," distinguishing it
from the western subspecies, "Audubon's Warbler," which has
the same markings, but is darker overall with a yellow instead of
white throat and lacks the white eyebrow of the Myrtle. Once
thought to be separate species, this changed when research
showed that they readily hybridize where ranges overlap.

Breeding | Adult male

BLACK-AND-WHITE WARBLER

Mniotilta varia L 5¼" (13 cm)

FIELD MARKS
Boldly striped on head, most of
body, and undertail coverts

Male's throat and cheeks are
black in breeding plumage;
in winter, chin is white

Females and immatures have
pale cheeks

Behavior
The only warbler that creeps around branches and up
and down tree trunks, foraging like a nuthatch; though
it does not use its tail to prop up its body. Probes
crevices in the bark of trees with its long bill for insects,
caterpillars, and spiders. Song is a long series of high,
thin *wee-see* notes; calls include a sharp *chip* and a high
seep-seep. If disturbed at nest, female drags wings on
the ground with tail spread for distraction.

Habitat
Prefers forests, both deciduous and mixed woolands, as
well as forested margins of swamps and rivers. Nests on
the ground, close to the base of a bush or tree, or in the
hollow of a stump or log.

Local Sites
Often easy to see and identify, the Black-and-white is a
winter resident throughout the peninsula and the Keys,
favoring oak and scrub oak forests. Look for it migrating down the Atlantic seaboard in early fall.

FIELD NOTES Once referred to as the Black-and-white Creeper
because of its creeper- or nuthatch-like feeding behavior, it
returns to northern breeding grounds much earlier than many
other warblers; it does not have to wait for leaves to develop to
load up on protein before the migration.

Year-round | Adult

PINE WARBLER

Dendroica pinus L 5¼" (14 cm)

FIELD MARKS
Yellow throat color extends onto
sides of neck and breast

Male is greenish-olive above with
dark streaks on sides of breast

Belly and undertail coverts white

Female is duller overall

Behavior
Will feed on ground and along branches for insects,
seeds, grapes, and berries, but forages mainly in trees,
gleaning insects, caterpillars, and spiders from bark,
leaves, and pine cones. Will also dive for flying insects.
Visits backyard feeders, especially for suet. Territorially
aggressive toward other species sharing the same stand
of pines, the Pine Warbler will partition its foraging
area into microhabitats according to height within a
tree, even inner-versus-outer branches. A very vocal
bird, its song is a twittering musical trill, varying in
speed. Call is slurred *tsup.*

Habitat
Favors open stands of pine trees, especially during
breeding season, but tends to winter throughout much
of its breeding range anyway. Conceals nest among the
needles at tips of pine branches. Also in mixed woodlands throughout range in winter.

Local Sites
A common and abundant resident of pine forests
throughout the state, but an irregular visitor to the
southern tip and the Keys.

FIELD NOTES In the winter, the Pine Warbler may be seen feeding
in mixed flocks with Eastern Bluebirds and pipits.

Year-round | Adult male

AMERICAN REDSTART

Setophaga ruticilla L 5¼" (13 cm)

FIELD MARKS

Male is glossy black overall

Bright orange patches on sides, wings, and tail

White belly and undertail coverts

Female gray-olive above; white below with yellow patches

Behavior

Often fans its tail and spreads its wings when perched, then leaps forth suddenly to hawk flying insects. Also gleans insects, caterpillars, spiders, berries, fruit, and seeds from branches and foliage. Sings often, even in midday heat, in a series of high, thin notes generally followed by a single, wheezy, downslurred note.

Habitat

Common in deciduous and mixed woodlands with viable understory, also in riparian and second-growth woodlands. Nests solitarily in forks of trees or bushes generally ten to twenty feet from ground in construction combining grasses, bark, roots, lichens, spider webs, and feathers.

Local Sites

A winter visitor to the Keys and the southern end of the peninsula, look for the Redstart as far north as the banks of the Caloosahatchee River.

FIELD NOTES An immature male resembles a female. By the first spring, it has gained black lores and some black spotting on the breast, though it still looks more like a female. A year-old redstart trying to breed in this plumage is at a great disadvantage, as he is immediately regarded as on the low end of the totem pole. It is not until his second fall that he acquires full adult plumage.

Year-round | Adult female

COMMON YELLOWTHROAT

Geothlypis trichas L 5" (13 cm)

FIELD MARKS

Adult male shows broad, black mask bordered above by light gray

Bright yellow throat and breast

Undertail coverts yellow

Female lacks black mask, has whitish eye ring

Behavior

Generally remains close to ground, skulking and hiding itself in overgrowth. May also be seen climbing vertically on stems. While foraging, hops on ground to glean insects, caterpillars, and spiders from foliage, twigs, and grass. Sometimes gleans while hovering or gives chase to flying insects.

Habitat

Stays low in grassy fields, shrubs, and marshes. Solitary nester atop piles of weed and grass or in small shrubs. Female builds nest alone from dried grasses and leaves, stems, pieces of bark, and hair.

Local Sites

A year-round resident across the panhandle, throughout the peninsula, and into the keys, and one of the most numerous and widespread of the warblers, look for the Yellowthroat hopping through your backyard.

FIELD NOTES The colors of the Yellowthroat vary widely according to geography. These differences reveal themselves in the amount of yellow on the underparts, the extent of olive shading on the upperparts, and the color of the border between mask and crown, which can go from stark white to gray. The southwestern race, *Geothlypis trichas chyseola*, is the brightest below and shows the most yellow.

Year-round | Adult female

EASTERN TOWHEE

Pipilo erythrophthalmus L 7½" (19 cm)

FIELD MARKS

Male shows black upperparts

Rufous sides, white underparts

Distinct white patch at base of primaries; distinct white tertials

Females similarly patterned, but black areas replaced by brown

Behavior

Remains low to ground, often scratching it with its feet together, head held low, and tail up. This exposes seeds and insects such as beetles and caterpillars, on which the Towhee feeds. Also forages for grasshoppers, spiders, moths, salamanders, and fruit. Known to choose an exposed perch to let out its song of *drink your tea*, sometimes shortened to just *drink tea*. Also calls in a clear, even-pitched, upslurred *swee*.

Habitat

Prefers partial to second-growth woodlands, with dense shrubs, brushy thickets, and extensive leaf litter. Also seen in brambly fields, hedgerows, and forest breaks. The Florida subspecies, *alleni*, favors especially coastal scrub, sand dune ridges, and pinelands.

Local Sites

Look for the *alleni* subspecies of the Eastern Towhee at woodland edges and along the banks of rivers year-round throughout Florida. The rustle of dry leaves underfoot is a great giveaway.

FIELD NOTES The subspecies found in the Florida peninsula, *Pipilo erythrophthalmus alleni*, is smaller in all measurements than more northern counterparts; it is also paler, duller, has less white in its wings and tail, and has straw-colored eyes.

Breeding | Adult

CHIPPING SPARROW

Spizella passerina L 5½" (14 cm)

FIELD MARKS
Breeding adult shows bright chestnut crown

Distinct white eyebrow

Black line extending from bill through eye to ear

Gray nape, cheek, and rump

Behavior
In summer, forages mainly on ground for insects; feeds mainly on seeds and agricultural grain in winter, oftentimes in family groups or mixed-species foraging flocks of towhees and other sparrows. A clever strategy employed by the Chipping Sparrow is to land atop a reed, bending it to the ground by the force of its weight, husking the seeds in the process. Song is a one-pitched, rapid-fire trill of dry *chip* notes. Calls in flight or when perched in a high, hard *seep* or *tsik*.

Habitat
Very adaptable, the Chipping Sparrow can be found in suburban gardens, city parks, woodlands, orchards, farms and fields. Rarely nests on the ground, preferring branches or vine tangles.

Local Sites
Spends winters on the peninsula and occasionally breeds in the panhandle. One of the tamest of sparrows, when your paths cross, it will most likely take food directly from your hand.

FIELD NOTES The Chipping Sparrow was probably one of the most common "city sparrows," until it was displaced from this habitat by the more aggressive House Sparrow, introduced to the U.S. from England.

Year-round | Adult male

NORTHERN CARDINAL

Cardinalis cardinalis L 8¾" (22 cm)

FIELD MARKS
Conspicuous crest

Cone-shaped reddish bill

Male is red overall with black face

Female is buffy brown tinged with
red on wings, crest, and tail

Juvenile browner overall

Behavior
Forages on the ground or low in shrubs for a wide
variety of insects, but mainly feeds on seeds, leaf buds,
berries, and fruit. Readily visits backyard feeders and
prefers sunflower seeds. Aggressive in defending its
territory, the Northern Cardinal will attack not only
other birds, but also itself, reflected in windows, rear-
view mirrors, chrome surfaces, and hubcaps. Sings a
variety of melodious songs year-round, including a *cue
cue cue*, a *cheer cheer cheer*, and a *purty purty purty*.

Habitat
Year-round resident in suburban gardens, city parks,
woodland edges, streamside thickets, and practically
any environment that provides thick, brushy cover for
feeding and nesting. Nests in forks of trees and bushes,
or in tangles of twigs and vines.

Local Sites
Abundant throughout the state, though slightly less
common in the Keys. Listen for courtship duets while
breeding occurs in spring and summer throughout the
state, though slightly less common in the Keys.

FIELD NOTES A non-migratory songbird, the Northern Cardinal
has adapted so well to landscaped yards and backyard feeders
that it continues to expand its range northward into Canada and
into the desert Southwest.

Breeding | Adult male

BLUE GROSBEAK

Passerina caerulea L 6¾" (17 cm)

FIELD MARKS
Breeding male plumage is blue overall

Wide chestnut wing bars

Large, heavy bill

Female is brownish overall, with chestnut wing bars and heavy bill

Behavior
Forages by hopping around on the ground for insects, snails, fruit, grain, and seeds. Will fly from perch to hawk insects in mid-air, and occasionally hovers to glean insects from leaves and twigs. Has a habit of twitching and spreading its tail. Distinctive call is a loud, explosive *chink*. Song is a full-bodied series of rising and falling warbles.

Habitat
Any low, brushy habitat along a roadway, stream, golf course, marsh, or woodland edge, especially near water. Nests low in trees, bushes, or clumps of weed.

Local Sites
Most abundant in spring and summer, especially in the panhandle and northern Florida. Known to breed in the Deer Point Lake region west of Panama City and the Paynes Prairie State Preserve south of Gainesville. Visit Kingsley Plantation on Fort George Island east of Jacksonville for migratory grosbeaks.

FIELD NOTES During long-distance migrations over open water to reach their wintering spots in Central and South America, Blue Grosbeaks are susceptible to displacement by weather systems, in the most extreme of cases finding themselves as far away as the British Isles.

Breeding | Adult male

INDIGO BUNTING

Passerina cyanea L 5½" (14 cm)

FIELD MARKS
Breeding male's plumage is deep blue overall

Female is brownish with diffuse streaking on breast and flanks

Body and bill smaller than Blue Grosbeak's

Behavior
In spring and summer, forages for insects from ground level to canopy, switching to a mainly seed and berry diet in the fall and winter. Sings in a series of varied phrases, usually paired, *sweet sweet* or *here here*, often with a trilled ending. Uses its heavy conical bill to crack or hull seeds. In winter, Indigo Buntings form feeding flocks, which may include thousands of birds, such as other buntings, sparrows, and finches.

Habitat
Prefers edges and bushy transition zones between old fields and woodlands. Range is the greatest of all buntings, extending northward to the edge of boreal forests.

Local Sites
Inhabits the entire peninsula but most readily seen in spring and summer in the Panhandle and northern Florida. Breeding Indigo Buntings are often observed on the La Chua Trail in Paynes Prairie State Preserve south of Gainesville and near the rivers and lakes around Apalachicola.

FIELD NOTES Male Indigo and Lazuli Buntings in their second year appear to learn their songs from neighboring males rather than from male parents. In overlapping areas, the two species may sing elements of each others' songs.

Year-round | Adult male

PAINTED BUNTING

Passerina ciris L 5½" (14 cm)

FIELD MARKS

Adult male has purple-blue head, red breast and rump, green back

Adult male's gaudy colors retained year-round

Female is bright green above, paler yellow-green below

Behavior

Courtship display is a mutual lopsided pose in which male and female tilt toward one another, exposing their bellies. Males puff up feathers and perform before females in a herky-jerky motion. Males are feisty and may draw blood—or even fight to the death—to defend territory. May mate with females other than primary partner. Males sing from exposed perches; their distinctive call is a loud, rich *chip.*

Habitat

Frequent vegetated habitats, riverbank thickets, woodland edges, and scrubby areas of the temperate through tropical areas in North and South America. Cup-shaped nests are well-concealed in shrubs, thickets, streamside brush, and trees.

Local Sites

While the Painted Bunting lives primarily in Texas, and its numbers are low in the East, it still breeds in the northeast corner of Florida, near the Georgia border. Winter range is extensive across the southern tip of the peninsula.

FIELD NOTES Often called the most colorful bird in North America, the Painted Bunting's bewitching plumage and melodious song has led to its being one of the most widely trapped and traded species.

Breeding | Adult *argutula*

EASTERN MEADOWLARK

Sturnella magna L 9½" (24 cm)

FIELD MARKS
Pointed bill

Black V-shaped breast
band

Yellow underparts

Outer tail feathers flash white
in flight

Behavior
Strong, direct flight, during which its call is a high, buzzy *drzzt*, given in a rapid series. Flicks its tail open and shut while foraging on the ground, feeding mainly on insects during spring and summer, seeds and agricultural grain in late fall and winter. Forms small flocks in winter. Constructs a domed nest on the ground that is often woven into the surrounding live grasses. Male known to brood while female starts second nest. Song is a clear *see-you-see-yeeer*.

Habitat
Prefers the open space offered by pastures, prairies, and farm fields. Common in fields and meadows. Listen for its rich, musical territorial songs that carry across the open grassland habitats it frequents.

Local Sites
Occurs throughout the peninsula but scarce in the Keys. Most abundant in the dry flatlands north and west of Lake Okeechobee. Also inhabits open areas near golf courses and agricultural operations.

FIELD NOTES The Eastern Meadowlark population has been slowly declining in the eastern states during the past few decades as its prime habitats are sacrificed to suburban sprawl, though its breeding range has been advancing northward.

Year-round | Adult male

RED-WINGED BLACKBIRD

Agelaius phoeniceus L 8¾" (22 cm)

FIELD MARKS

Male is glossy black

Bright red shoulder patches broadly edged with buffy yellow

Wings slightly rounded at tips

Females are dark brown above, heavily streaked below

Behavior

The male's bright red shoulder patches are usually visible when it sings from a perch, often atop a cattail or tall grass stalk, defending its territory. At other times only the yellow border may be visible. Territorially aggressive, a male's social status is dependent on the amount of red he displays on his shoulders. Runs and hops while foraging for insects, grass seeds ,and agricultural grain in pastures and open fields, sometimes considered a threat to crops. Song is a liquid, gurgling *konk-la-reee*, ending in a trill. Call is a *chack* note.

Habitat

Found breeding colonially mainly in freshwater marshes with thick vegetation. Nests in cattails, bushes, or dense grass near water. During winter, males and females flock together and forage in wooded swamps and farm fields.

Local Sites

A permanent Florida resident, found throughout the state, especially in freshwater marshes and swamps.

FIELD NOTES Breeding males often have more than one mate and therefore spend less time caring for young than do the females. Very often the majority of blackbirds in large winter flocks are Red-winged Blackbirds.

Year-round | Adult male *versicolor*

COMMON GRACKLE

Quiscalus quiscula L 12½" (32 cm)

FIELD MARKS
Long, keel-shaped tail

Pale yellow eyes

Plumage appears all black; in
good light, males show glossy
purplish blue head, neck, breast

Pointed beak

Behavior
Often nests in small colonies and flocks to large, noisy,
communal roosts in the evening. Mainly seen on the
ground in a group, feeding on insects, spiders, grubs,
and earthworms. Grackles will also wade into shallow
water to forage for minnows and crayfish. Will feast on
eggs and baby birds. Usually mates for life. Courtship
display consists of male puffing out shoulder feathers
to make a collar, drooping his wings, and singing. Birds
produce sounds like ripping cloth or cracking twigs.
Call note is a loud *chuck*.

Habitat
Prefers open spaces provided by farm fields, pastures,
marshes, and suburban yards and gardens, and requires
wooded areas, especially conifers, for nesting and
roosting.

Local Sites
Abundant and gregarious, roams in mixed flocks in
open fields, marshes, parks, and suburban areas
throughout the peninsula.

FIELD NOTES The closely related Boat-
tailed Grackle, *Quiscalus major* (inset),
at 16 1/2" (42 cm) is larger than the
Common Grackle and has a rounder
crown and duller, brownish eyes.

Year-round | Adult male

BROWN-HEADED COWBIRD

Molothrus ater L 7½" (19 cm)

FIELD MARKS
Pointed bill

Male's brown head contrasts with
metallic green-black body

Female is gray-brown above,
paler below

Strong, direct flight

Behavior
Cowbirds often forage on the ground among herds
of cattle, feeding on the insects flushed by the grazing
farm animals. They also feed on grass seeds and agricultural grain. Generally feed with tails cocked up.
Travel and roost in large flocks after breeding. Song
is a squeaky, gurgling call that includes a squeaky whistle. All cowbirds are nest parasites and lay their eggs
in the nests of other species, leaving the responsibilites
of feeding and fledging of young to the host birds.

Habitat
Cowbirds prefer the open habitat provided by
farmlands, pastures, prairies and edgelands bordering
woods and forests. Also found in general around
human habitation.

Local Sites
Ranges throughout Florida, in woodlands, farmlands, and suburbs.

FIELD NOTES The Shiny Cowbird, *Molothrus
bonariensis* (inset), is a South American
native that spread through the
Caribbean Islands and Cuba and
arrived in Florida in 1985. It is not common in southern
coastal Florida or on the Gulf Coast. The male is blackish with
a glossy purple head, breast, and back.

Year-round | Adult female

ORCHARD ORIOLE

Icterus spurius L 7¼" (18 cm)

FIELD MARKS
Male is chestnut overall with black hood

Female is olive above, yellowish below

Bill is slightly decurved

First-year male has black bib

Behavior
Forages by inserting thin, sharply pointed bill into holes and crevices. Forages as well fairly high up in trees and bushes, hopping from branch to branch. Courtship includes female wing drooping and male bowing, repeatedly showing colors. Males arrive at breeding ground before females and begin to sing to attract a mate. Pairs mate for one season. Call is sharp *chuck*. Song is a loud, rapid burst of whistled notes, downslurred at end, which varies considerably from song to song.

Habitat
Locally common in suburban shade trees and orchards, Orchard Orioles forage in trees and shrubs. In arid spots they may glean insects and nectar from cacti. In wooded areas, females build pouch-shaped nests, woven from grasses, hair, and moss, and hung on branches too fragile to support predators.

Local Sites
Found in the summer months in the upper half of the peninsula and throughout the Panhandle.

FIELD NOTES Unlike most songbirds, orioles have a unique jaw musculature that allows them both to open and close their bill forcefully. Called "gaping," this practice allows them to pry into crevices or soft bark and expose prey hidden to other birds.

Year-round | Adult male

HOUSE FINCH

Carpodacus mexicanus L 6" (15 cm)

FIELD MARKS

Male has brown cap

Front of head, bib, and rump typically red, but can be orange or, occasionally, yellow

Bib set off from streaked underparts

Female brown-streaked overall

Behavior

A seed eater. Has undulating flight, in which square tail is apparent. In nonbreeding season, spirals overhead while traveling in flocks. Crossed bills allow House Finches to wedge open conifer cones and extract seed with their tongues. Acrobatic foragers, they hang upside down to reach seeds or buds. Lively, high-pitched song, usually ending in a nasal *wheer*. Calls include a whistled *wheat*.

Habitat

Wooded areas or suburban and urban areas where they may nest on buildings.

Local Sites

Found in upper half of the peninsula and throughout the Panhandle. Especially numerous in towns. In autumn, flocks of "winter finches" roam from northern climes to Florida and vicinity.

FIELD NOTES As with many other songbirds, finches appear to be monogamous. The male defends territory around the female. The paired male chases another male only when it approaches the mate.

Nonbreeding | Adult female

AMERICAN GOLDFINCH

Carduelis tristis L 5" (13 cm)

FIELD MARKS

Male bright yellow with black cap,
female duller over all, lacks cap

Black wings have white bars,
male has yellow shoulder patch

White uppertail and undertail
coverts

Behavior

This gregarious and active bird is often seen spiraling
overhead as it travels in flocks during the nonbreeding
season. Flocks may contain a hundred or more birds
and include several species. Distinctive flight call is
per-chik-o-ree. These acrobatic foragers hang upside
down to reach seeds or buds. Visit bird feeders when
natural food is scarce. The finch diet, heavily seeds and
vegetable matter, is the most vegetarian of any North
American bird, but sometimes eats insects. Song is
lively series of trills, twitters, and *swee* notes.

Habitat

Found in weedy fields, open second-growth woodlands, roadsides. Especially seeks territory rich in
thistles and sunflowers.

Local Sites

In winter, find the American Goldfinch throughout
the peninsula and Panhandle, having migrated from
the North, as far away as Canada.

FIELD NOTES Sometimes a cowbird will lay its eggs in the nest
of an American Goldfinch. Although the eggs will hatch, most
young cowbirds die before they leave the nest, due to their
inability to obtain enough protein from the finch's seed diet.

Breeding | Adult male

HOUSE SPARROW

Passer domesticus L 6¼" (16 cm)

FIELD MARKS
Black bill, black bib

Male breeding plumage has gray crown

Chestnut nape, back, shoulders

Female has streaked back, buffy eyestripe, unstreaked breast

Behavior
Abundant and aggressive, gregarious in winter. Feeds on grains, seeds, and shoots, or seeks out bird feeders for sunflower seeds or millet. Also forages on the ground, getting food from plants or animal dung. In urban areas, House Sparrows may beg for food from humans and will clean up any crumbs left behind. Singing males give persistent cheep. Breeding occurs in the first year, and pairs mate for life. Females choose mates mostly according to song display.

Habitat
Found in close proximity to humans. Can be observed in urban and suburban areas and in rural landscapes inhabited by humans and livestock.

Local Sites
These nonmigrating birds span the peninsula and Panhandle year-round. Found in all cities, suburbs, and populated agricultural areas.

FIELD NOTES In mating ritual, the male stiffly profiles for the female by fanning its cocked tail, sticking out its chest, drooping its wings slightly, and calling repeatedly as it hops around. Other males may gather and compete by chasing the female.

Mostly Black

Muscovy Duck, 14

Magnificent Frigatebird, 32

Double-Crested Cormorant, 38

Anhinga, 40

Turkey Vulture, 66

American Crow, 186

European Starling, 218

American Redstart, 228

Eastern Towhee, 232

Red-winged Blackbird, 246

Common Grackle, 248

Brown-headed Cowbird, 250

Mostly Black and White

Canada Goose, 12

Common Loon, 28

Swallow-tailed Kite, 72

American Oystercatcher, 108

Ruddy Turnstone, 118

Laughing Gull, 128

Royal Tern, 134

Forster's Tern, 136

Black Skimmer, 140

Red-Bellied Woodpecker, 166

Downy Woodpecker, 170

Red-Cockaded Woodpecker, 172

 Pileated Woodpecker, 174

 Barn Swallow, 192

 Black-and-White Warbler, 224

 Eastern Bluebird, 208

 Blue Grosbeak, 238

Mostly Blue

 Little Blue Heron, 48

 Indigo Bunting, 240

 Tri-colored Heron, 50

Mostly Brown

 Yellow-crowned Night-Heron, 58

 Fulvous Whistling-Duck, 10

 Rock Pigeon, 142

 Blue-winged Teal, 22

 Belted Kingfisher, 164

 Northern Bobwhite, 24

 Blue Jay, 182

 Wild Turkey, 26

 Florida Scrub-Jay, 184

 Pied-billed Grebe, 30

Tree Swallow, 188

Brown Pelican, 36

Purple Martin, 190

 Osprey, 70

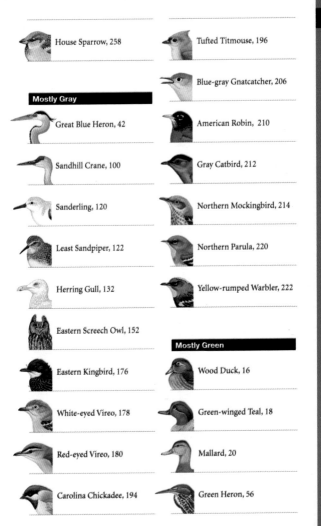

The main entry for each species is listed in **boldface** type and refers to the text page opposite the illustration.

A check-off box is provided next to each common-name entry so that you can use this index as a checklist of the species you have identified.

ACKNOWLEDGMENTS

The Book Division would like to thank the following people for their guidance and contribution in creating the National Geographic *Field Guide to Birds: Florida*

Cortez C. Austin, Jr.:
Cortez Austin is a wildlife photographer who specializes in North American and tropical birds. An ardent conservationist, he has donated images and given lectures for conservation groups and has published articles and photographs in U.S. birding magazines. His photographs have appeared in field guides, books, and brochures.

Bates Littlehales:
A National Geographic photographer for more than 30 years covering myriad subjects around the globe, Bates Littlehales continues to specialize in photographing birds and is an expert in capturing their beauty and ephemeral nature. He is co-author of the *National Geographic Field Guide to Photography: Birds.*

Rulon Simmons:
Co-author of the *National Geographic Field Guide to Photography: Birds* with Bate Littlehales, Rulon Simmons is a technical expert with Eastman Kodak, where he works with imaging systems for aircraft and satellites. Combining this skill with his passion for birding, he photographs species across North America.

Brian Sullivan:
Birding travels and field projects have taken Brian Sullivan to Central and South America, to the Arctic and across North America. He has written and consulted on books and popular and scientific literature on North American birds. Research interests include migration, sea birds, raptors, and bird identification. He is a Field Coordinator for the endangered San Clemente Loggerhead Shrike Recovery Project.

Tom Vezo:
Tom Vezo is an award-winning wildlife photographer who is widely published throughout the U.S.and Europe. He specializes in bird photography but photographs other wildlife and nature subjects as well. Please visit Tom at his website www.tomvezo.com.

Peter Wallack:
Peter Wallack has been behind a camera since 1972. He has photographed subjects from landscapes to third world cultures. Peter and his wife, Ruth, retired to Sanibel Island in 2002 for its beauty and for the birds inhabiting this island and the opportunities to photograph them. To see more of his images go to www.birdsofsanibel.com

Cover Peter Wallack; 2 Bates Littlehales; 10 Bates Littlehales; 12 Bates Littlehales; 14 Peter Wallack; 16 Cortez C. Austin Jr.; 18 Cortez C. Austin Jr.; 20 Bates Littlehales; 22 Bates Littlehales; 24 Cortez C. Austin Jr.; 26 Cortez C. Austin Jr.; 28 Michael Quinton, NGS Image Sales; 30 Cortez C. Austin Jr.; 32 Brian Sullivan; 34 Bates Littlehales; 36 Tim Zurowski/CORBIS; 38 Peter Wallack; 40 Cortez C. Austin Jr.; 42 Bates Littlehales; 44 Cortez C. Austin Jr.; 46 Peter Wallack; 48 Peter Wallack; 50 Peter Wallack; 52 Cortez C. Austin Jr.; 54 Cortez C. Austin Jr.; 56 Peter Wallack; 58 Cortez C. Austin Jr.; 60 Peter Wallack; 62 Peter Wallack; 64 Peter Wallack; 66 Bates Littlehales; 68 Peter Wallack; 70 Cortez C. Austin Jr.; 72 Joe McDonald/CORBIS; 74 Brian Sullivan; 76 Cortez C. Austin Jr.; 78 Brian Sullivan; 80 Peter Wallack; 82 Cortez C. Austin Jr.; 84 Cortez C. Austin Jr.; 86 Cortez C. Austin Jr.; 88 Bates Littlehales; 90 Joe McDonald/CORBIS; 92 Cortez C. Austin Jr.; 94 Peter Wallack; 96 Cortez C. Austin Jr.; 98 Bates Littlehales; 100 Bates Littlehales; 102 Tim Zurowski/CORBIS; 104 Peter Wallack; 106 Cortez C. Austin Jr.; 108 Cortez C. Austin Jr.; 110 Bates Littlehales; 112 Bates Littlehales; 114 Bates Littlehales; 116 Peter Wallack; 118 Peter Wallack; 120 Peter Wallack; 122 Brian Sullivan; 124 Bates Littlehales; 126 Peter Wallack; 128 Cortez C. Austin Jr.; 130 Cortez C. Austin Jr.; 132 Cortez C. Austin Jr.; 134 Brian Sullivan; 136 Cortez C. Austin Jr.; 138 Brian Sullivan; 140 Cortez C. Austin Jr.; 142 Cortez C. Austin Jr.; 144 Cortez C. Austin Jr.; 146 Cortez C. Austin Jr.; 148 Bates Littlehales; 150 Bates Littlehales; 152 Cortez C. Austin Jr.; 154 Cortez C. Austin Jr.; 156 Cortez C. Austin Jr.; 158 Bates Littlehales; 160 Lynda Richardson/CORBIS; 162 Bates Littlehales; 164 Cortez C. Austin Jr.; 166 Peter Wallack; 168 Bates Littlehales; 170 Bates Littlehales; 172 Bates Littlehales; 174 Bates Littlehales; 176 Cortez C. Austin Jr.; 178 Bates Littlehales; 180 Bates Littlehales; 182 Bates Littlehales; 184 Cortez C. Austin Jr.; 186 Bates Littlehales; 188 Cortez C. Austin Jr.; 190 Rulon Simmons; 192 Cortez C. Austin Jr.; 194 Bates Littlehales; 196 Bates Littlehales; 198 Gary W. Carter/CORBIS; 200 Cortez C. Austin Jr.; 202 Bates Littlehales; 204 Bates Littlehales; 206 Ron Austin; Frank Lane Picture Agency/CORBIS; 208 Cortez C. Austin Jr.; 210 Bates Littlehales; 212 Cortez C. Austin Jr.; 214 Cortez C. Austin Jr.; 216 Rulon Simmons; 218 Cortez C. Austin Jr.; 220 Tom Vezo; 222 Bates Littlehales; 224 Bates Littlehales; 226 Tom Vezo; 228 Bates Littlehales; 230 Bates Littlehales; 232 Bates Littlehales; 234 Bates Littlehales; 236 Cortez C. Austin Jr.; 238 Cortez C. Austin Jr.; 240 Bates Littlehales; 242 Bates Littlehales; 244 Cortez C. Austin Jr.; 246 Cortez C. Austin Jr.; 248 Rulon Simmons; 250 Tom Vezo; 252 Lynda Richardson/CORBIS; 254 Bates Littlehales; 256 Bates Littlehales; 258 Cortez C. Austin Jr.

FIELD NOTES

NATIONAL GEOGRAPHIC
FIELD GUIDE TO BIRDS:
FLORIDA

Edited by Mel Baughman

**Published by
the National Geographic Society**

John M. Fahey, Jr.,
President and Chief Executive Officer

Gilbert M. Grosvenor,
Chairman of the Board

Nina D. Hoffman,
Executive Vice President

Prepared by the Book Division

Kevin Mulroy,
Vice President and Editor-in-Chief

Charles Kogod, *Illustrations Director*

Marianne R. Koszorus, *Design Director*

Barbara Brownell Grogan,
Executive Editor

Staff for this Book

Barbara Brownell Grogan, *Project Editor*

Carol Norton, *Art Director*

Melissa Farris, *Design Consultant*

Sharon Berry, *Illustrations Editor*

Dan O'Toole, Mary Jo Slazak, *Writers*

Susan Tyler Hitchcock, *Text Editor*

Carl Mehler, *Director of Maps*

Mel Baughman, Matt Chwastyk,
Dan O'Toole, Mapping Specialists,
Map Research and Production

Rick Wain, *Production Project Manager*

Manufacturing and Quality Control

Christopher A. Liedel,
Chief Financial Officer

Phillip L. Schlosser, *Managing Director*

John T. Dunn, *Technical Director*

One of the world's largest nonprofit scientific and educational organizations, the National Geographic Society was founded in 1888 "for the increase and diffusion of geographic knowledge." Fulfilling this mission, the Society educates and inspires millions every day through its magazines, books, television programs, videos, maps and atlases, research grants, the National Geographic Bee, teacher workshops, and innovative classroom materials. The Society is supported through membership dues, charitable gifts, and income from the sale of its educational products. This support is vital to National Geographic's mission to increase global understanding and promote conservation of our planet through exploration, research, and education.

For more information, please call
1-800-NGS LINE (647-5463) or write
to the following address:

National Geographic Society
1145 17th Street N.W.
Washington, D.C. 20036-4688 U.S.A.

Visit the Society's Web site at
www.nationalgeographic.com.

**Library of Congress
Cataloging-in-Publication Data**

Available upon request.